TOO MUCH MUCH CRAZY

also by tom tomorrow

TOO MUCH CRAZY

by tom tomorrow

Soft Skull Press
New York

Copyright © 2011 by Tom Tomorrow (Dan Perkins)
Foreword © 2011 by Michael Moore

Library of Congress Cataloging-in-Publication Data

Tomorrow, Tom, 1961-
 Too much crazy / Tom Tomorrow.
     p. cm.

ISBN 978-1-59376-410-4

1. American wit and humor, Pictorial. 2. United States—Politics and government—Caricatures and cartoons. I. Title.

PN6727.T66T66 2010
741.5'973—dc22
                            2010035944

Cover design by Dan Perkins
Interior layout by Neuwirth & Associates
Printed in China

Soft Skull Press
An Imprint of Counterpoint LLC
1919 Fifth Street
Berkeley, CA 94710

www.softskull.com
www.counterpointpress.com

www.thismodernworld.com
www.twitter.com/tomtomorrow
www.facebook.com/TomTomorrowFB

Distributed by Publishers Group West

10 9 8 7 6 5 4 3 2 1

For Beverly and Nicholas—

the downstairs guy thanks you

After decades of fighting the forces of evil, Tom Tomorrow was looking forward to a well-deserved rest. With the historic election of Barack Obama to the White House, and the Bush/Cheney crime family permanently retired, Tom and Sparky could finally explore other facets of their cartoon lives. We, the fans, looked forward to strips about the little things in life that are *really* funny—nagging wives, nitwit sidekicks, knee-slapping cubicle humor.

But then something strange happened. Instead of ending the war, the new president tripled the number of troops in Afghanistan and decided to leave 50,000 "advisors" in Iraq. In the coming attractions category, U.S. military force was expanded in Pakistan, the horn of Africa, Yemen, and Columbia. And an Army whistleblower who posted video on the Internet of possible American war crimes was arrested instead of rewarded.

On the economic battlefield, instead of being prosecuted and jailed, the thieves on Wall Street who collapsed the economy got to keep their jobs, their bonuses, and their ability to bring about the next crash. Pharmaceutical companies breathed a sigh of relief when they were offered a deal that left them out of the health care reform bill—and millions of Americans remained uncovered should they get sick.

Daily newspapers started to fold, tens of thousands of teachers lost their jobs, and 40 million adult Americans were now considered to be functional illiterates.

And the Republican Party, instead of joining in to help clean up the mess they made, just got weirder and weirder. They started dressing up in strange costumes and holding "tea parties." Tea? The drink of sissies? I began to miss the rednecks of old. Of course these new Republicans were still every bit as racist—and it's clear they are not going to go away until the doctor who delivered baby Barack in Hawaii comes forward with the proof and placenta.

So . . . as the nation spiraled out of control, and many believed the next president would be a moose hunter from Alaska, Tom Tomorrow could not put away his sharp colored pens. Sparky could not retire to the Hamptons. America—and the world—needed them more than ever.

This book chronicles the first two years of Obama's America as seen through the eyes of Tom Tomorrow. At a time when newspapers are dropping their cartoons—especially the politically-tinged ones—we are lucky to have this collection printed and in our hands. The future for such satire seems perilous. These strips should exist as Exhibit A, proving why we need Tom Tomorrow and every cartoonist like him. The wars aren't going to end on their own. The rich will not let up until they have us all in hock and are holding our children for ransom. Who is fighting for us? Who is slaying the bastards with ridicule and wit? Who simply doesn't care about whom he offends or what hand he bites that's feeding him?

The answer begins as you turn this page . . .

Michael Moore
Traverse City, Michigan
August 2010

introduction: when the levee breaks

It's a strange moment in the world, and in most people's lives (mine included, but we'll get back to that in a page or two). It feels like we're on the cusp of something, but no one's quite sure what. Politically things haven't worked out quite as well as we might have hoped a year and a half ago, and economically, well—I am reminded of the scene from *The Simpsons* in which Homer shakes his fist at the sky and declares triumphantly, "I'm Homer Simpson, the most powerful food critic in town, who will never get his comeuppance! You hear me? NO COMEUPPANCE!" It doesn't work out so well for Homer, and it hasn't worked out so well for us. Despite the hubris of those who insisted otherwise, it turns out you *can't* fight two wars while simultaneously cutting taxes for the wealthy and inflating a fantastical housing bubble, all while the Lords of Wall Street are manipulating the economy in ways that they themselves do not fully comprehend . . . without escaping a little comeuppance.

So here we are. And as they say on the blogs, no one could possibly have foreseen *this*.

And just to keep things interesting, now we've got the Tea Party and Michele Bachmann and Half-Term Palin and of course Crazy Glenn Beck, who recently released a thriller called *The Overton Window*. The title refers to a Secret Marxist Conspiracy to shift the window of acceptable public opinion to the far left in order to pave the way for a SECRET MARXIST

CONSPIRACY TAKEOVER. I believe they are uncredited, but the book was largely co-authored by The Voices in Glenn Beck's Head. Though in fairness, any impartial observer would have to concede that Glenn Beck himself *has* significantly shifted the Overton Window—of *crazy*. (Ba doom boom.) But really: a couple of years ago it would have been hard to imagine how pedestrian O'Reilly and Hannity and Limbaugh and the rest now look by comparison.

In case I'm not making my point clearly enough, there's some serious crazy out there these days, maybe more than I've ever seen. And I've been watching this stuff for a while now.

I haven't had a real job in more than twenty years, at least not the kind where you have to be in a certain place at a certain time, and, you know, do whatever it is people with jobs do. I'm not even sure what my last real job was—there was never a clear line of demarcation, a specific moment when I stood up abruptly and announced with great passion that some boss could take a particular job and shove it. My life in offices and art departments ended with a whimper rather than a bang; at some point I just finished up a day's work and said goodbye to the people I was working with, and never needed to go back again.

And that's no small thing, twenty years of independence. It came with its own price, of course, since everything does: in this case, a constant, inexorable weekly deadline hanging over my head like the sword of Damocles, defining the parameters of my life for every hour of every day of those twenty years. I survive from one idea to the next, and every week feels like a new battleground with me on one side and the entire world on the other.

But still: some people have *real* problems, you know?

One of the tricks to maintaining this kind of independence is to make sure that no single person has the power to derail your livelihood. You hedge your bets, keep your eggs in different baskets. And for quite a while, I thought I had that one figured out. I recoiled in horror at the thought of a staff job on a single newspaper. I syndicated my cartoon to as many papers as I could (mostly alternative weeklies), and if I lost the occasional paper now and then, well, there were still plenty of others. My eggs were in plenty of baskets. What I didn't count on was the baskets themselves merging.

Times were not good in the alt-weekly industry at the beginning of 2009. Papers were going out of business, and space was getting tighter in the rest (which is never good for cartoonists). And there was one other variable: as in most industries, a few big players had gradually become dominant over the years, and when two of the biggest consolidated into one, a lot of my eggs were suddenly in a single basket after all. And sure enough, in late January of that year, the phone rang. A honcho from the alt-weekly conglomerate in question was ever so sorry, but to save literally tens of dollars each week, they had decided to drop all cartoons across their entire chain, effective immediately.[1]

---

1 I eventually made it back into the chain's largest paper, but as of this writing, eighteen months later, remain locked out of the rest.

Let me pause to reiterate: there are people with real problems in this economy. A lot of them. Millions of people are out of work, losing their homes. As I write this introduction, Republicans have been holding unemployment benefits hostage, toying with the fate of the truly desperate in order to score cheap political points against Obama. So to keep things in perspective: I had a roof over my head, which I was (and am) in no danger of losing. I was still perfectly able to put "food on my family," in the immortal words of our previous President. And more to the point, I still had eighty or ninety papers, and a reasonably strong online presence. This wasn't a fatal blow—but it was bad enough. I lost a dozen of my largest cities in a single moment: New York, Minneapolis, Los Angeles, Seattle, Denver. It *felt* like a nuclear first strike on my career.

So I did what you do; I tried to fight back. I put out the word hoping to inspire reader protests and kick up a fuss. It rarely works—once a paper decides to drop you, they tend not to reverse the decision—but I didn't want to go down quietly. I mean, I've always been aware that tastes change and editors are fickle, and every additional year that I continue to make a living in this extremely unlikely manner is something of a gift. On the other hand, the alt-weeklies are undeniably the stewards of an art form that has grown up around them, a sub-genre of cartooning as distinct from mainstream comics as the blues from Beethoven. The extent to which they honor that stewardship will likely define the extent to which the art form continues to exist. As my friend Jen Sorensen put it recently, "Like bamboo-eating pandas, we alternative political cartoonists thrive in a very particular habitat—the free weekly newspaper—and we're rapidly becoming an endangered species."

Of course, at this point, I can see the question coming from a mile away: *Why* do you keep blathering on about *newspapers*? Who *cares* about the dead-tree media?

Here's the thing: I get a lot of earnest advice about how to make a living online, mostly from people who don't. The visionaries assure me that vast riches await those who have faith enough to distribute their work without thought of compensation. And maybe they're right. I hope they're right! Because the internet may be a cesspit governed by the standards of hyperactive amoral fourteen-year-old boys—but it's sure not going away.

I kid of course! Well, sort of. But I've had an online presence since the early nineties; I was one of the first cartoonists with a website and was—to the best of my knowledge—the very first cartoonist with a public email address. I was also one of the earliest pioneers of the liberal blogosphere[2], and at the moment, I have close to 10,000 followers on Twitter. So it's not exactly as if I'm standing on a lawn, yelling at kids to get off it. But the coin of the online realm is still mostly traffic and exposure, which my local grocers remain stubbornly reluctant to accept in exchange for their goods. With a couple of exceptions, alternative newspapers are still how I pay the bills.

---

2 I was even profiled in one of the very first articles ever to appear in *The New York Times* on the subject of blogging ("Is Weblog Technology Here to Stay or Just Another Fad?" Feb. 25, 2002). If you look up the print edition, you'll see a large photograph of me in front of my old CRT monitor. Because, you know, it was about the internet and stuff.

Maybe newspapers are a dying breed, maybe they're not—but as long as they're still being published, I want to be running in them. As my friend Derf says, "I don't want to be the appetizer course at the Donner Party." I'm just trying to hang in there as long as I can—which, when you think about it, is pretty much all any of us are doing in this life.

Okay? Okay.

So if cartooning is the ugly stepchild of American arts, then alt-weekly cartooning is the ugly stepchild's ugly stepchild.

Some amazing people have tried to make a go of this untenable thing over the years. Some lasted, some didn't. Before you had anybody, you had Jules Feiffer, the granddaddy of us all, in the *Voice*, in the very early days, and everybody who's come along since owes him an unimaginable debt of gratitude for setting this whole thing in motion. Later, in the late seventies, early eighties, when I was living in New York City, surviving on Ramen noodles and picking up the *Voice* when I could afford it (before they adopted the free weekly model), there was Mark Alan Stamaty's intricate, crazed *MacDoodle Street* (later *Washingtoon*), and Stan Mack's voyeuristic *Real Life Funnies*, each of which took up, Christ, it must have been half a page of newsprint. (Those were the glory days of alt-weekly cartooning, children, back before space became tight and cartoons were shrunk down so small you needed a magnifying glass to read them.) And then came the generation after that, the shining moment for the baby boomers in our little field, when the alt-weeklies really took off and made stars of Matt Groening and Lynda Barry. I was actually surprised to read in a recent *New York Times* profile that Lynda, at the height of her success, was only running in seventy-five papers—I'll probably hit seventy-five papers soon, but it will be on the way down. But Lynda was a rock star—she was a regular guest on Letterman, everyone knew who she was. And Matt—well, every human being on the planet has heard of *The Simpsons*, though for me, Matt will always first and foremost be the genius behind *Life in Hell*, one of a handful of cartoons that inspired me to do what I have done with my life.

In 1983, for a little while, I was living in a Chicago suburb, commuting into the city to a tedious temp job in the offices of a large advertising agency, and one of the things I looked forward to each week was the new issue of the incredibly comics-friendly *Chicago Reader*, which ran most of the pioneers of our little field: Matt and Lynda, and Charles Burns's *Dog Boy*, and I believe Gary Panter, and probably *The Angriest Dog in the World*—a strip by film director David Lynch, which literally consisted of the same three panels every week, with only a word balloon altered (foreshadowing David Rees's work, though the comparison is unfair to Rees, whose now-retired strip, *Get Your War On*, had infinitely more substance and wit).

Around the same time, I ran across the sublimely strange work of Norman Dog, whose strip ran in the *East Bay Express*, and who would later become a friend and studio mate for many years, after I moved west. (And damn, there were a lot of us in the Bay Area then. I didn't even really think about it that much, when a once-a-month cartoonists' drinking bash would fill a bar with fifty, a hundred cartoonists. It just seemed like the norm. Who *wouldn't* want to be a cartoonist?)

I loved it. I loved it all. And it was what I wanted to do. And I mean specifically cartoons for alt-weeklies: outside of the rigidly formatted daily newspaper comics page, but also outside of the comic shop ghetto, these papers gave you the chance of reaching an entirely different audience. And I was lucky enough—*incredibly* lucky enough—to make that happen, to carve out a space for myself. At the time, it felt like there wasn't any more room for new cartoons, that it was all over already. In retrospect it was actually the perfect moment, but you really never understand, when it's happening, how lucky you are to be just the right age at just the right time. Sure, the cartoonists of "my" wave were never going to be Jules Feiffer, would never have that dominance or ubiquity—*that* moment was over. Nor were we even going to be Matt-and-Lynda, the aforementioned dynamic duo who *owned* the weeklies throughout the eighties. But we did okay for ourselves: Derf, and Max Cannon, and myself, and Lloyd Dangle, and Ruben Bolling, and Ward Sutton and Ted Rall (though Ted was always something of a hybrid, running in as many dailies as he did weeklies). Keith Knight and Carol Lay. Tony Millionaire. Even my old friend Dave Eggers—before he became "Dave Eggers," he had a strip called *Smarter Feller* in the *SF Weekly*, which featured a talking handbag, among other things.

But the ones who came after us—if we're the buggy-whip makers, they're the buggy-whip interns, the ones who never really got their fair shot before history fucked us all. Jen Sorensen, Matt Bors, Brian McFadden, Mikhaela Reid, August Pollak—these would have been the next generation of alt-weekly stars, if the game hadn't changed so suddenly. And maybe more to the point, if the importance of cartoons to the alt-weekly press hadn't been increasingly ignored and forgotten and brushed aside as the years went on.[3]

Which is not to say these artists haven't had their own impact, or won't—just that it won't be via the alt-weeklies alone. Those days are gone.

Which brings us back to the bitter winter of 2009.

My career had just taken a hit, and I was trying to gin up reader protests—er, that is, to lay the groundwork for an entirely spontaneous grassroots reader uprising through my blog, through Twitter, and by emailing everyone I knew in the dozen cities where I'd lost a paper. In Seattle, that list included a friend of mine who's pretty famous, and I thought that if *he* were to write a letter to the local paper it might stir things up, get a little attention. And this is where the narrative of my life suddenly veered off in an entirely unexpected direction.

---

3 If I had a dime for every person who's told me over the past twenty years that cartoons are the main reason they bother to pick up these papers, I would have a very large pile of dimes. Which could come in handy, the way things are going.

You see, a month or so after the great Cartoon Apocalypse (as Max Cannon christened it) I got a call from my Seattle friend, who was, of course, BILL GATES. And he bought the newspaper chain in question, put me in charge, and now they run NOTHING BUT CARTOONS. And everyone got a free pony.

There I go again, with the kidding.

Actually my friend in Seattle was Eddie Vedder, which is almost as improbable, now that I think about it. (We'd met eight or nine years earlier, backstage at a Ralph Nader rally, and stayed loosely in touch over the years.) He was calling to say that he intended to write a letter of public support (which he later did), and also to suggest that maybe we could work together somehow—maybe I could do some posters for some Pearl Jam shows at some point (which I later would)[4], or maybe—he'd talked this over with the band, and everybody liked the idea— they were thinking maybe I could take a shot at doing their next album cover.

Which I gotta say, was not a bad consolation prize.

To quote something Eddie said to a newspaper reporter, after it was all said and done: "It used to be real simple. Dan writes a strip, it gets in the paper, people read it, Dan gets paid. That's how we felt too: We make records, people buy them at a record store, we tour, there you go. It's not that simple anymore."

---

4 A series of posters I designed for PJ's four-night run of shows closing out the Spectrum in Philadelphia are reproduced at the end of this book as a special bonus for you, the reader. And also because we had some extra pages to fill.

Now, the job wasn't a freebie, and it wasn't guaranteed. I still had to earn it, and if I hadn't come up with something that worked, they'd have gone off in some other direction entirely and that would have been that. But happily—and to compress the experience of an extraordinary year into a brief paragraph—it turned out to be one of those collaborations that just really click, and ultimately led to some of the stranger and more wonderful experiences of my life. I've worked with one of *the* great rock bands, hung out with them in their studio and watched them rehearse. (I'm even in the background of one of their videos, if you know where to look.) I've been invited to stand out on stage and take a bow in front of 20,000 fans. I've ridden in a police motorcade, and stayed up all night drinking wine and playing pool with my friend the rock star. And I've had my art displayed prominently in every Target store in the nation, which may have been the most surreal thing of all.[5]

And while I will probably never win a Pulitzer, I do have a framed gold record hanging on my wall[6], and how many cartoonists can say that?

---

5 As part of their own attempt to negotiate the post-internet world, Pearl Jam cut a deal making Target the exclusive big-box retailer for the new album, *Backspacer*. (This was more than a year before the company made their notorious contribution to an anti-gay politician in Minnesota.)

6 Presented to me in an impromptu ceremony backstage at Madison Square Garden. It was a good evening.

As the noted philosophers Sonny and Cher once sagely observed, the beat goes on. You never know where things are going to lead. You can make yourself crazy worrying about it, or you can just enjoy the ride. In a weird way, getting cut from those papers was one of the best things that ever happened to me. If some trickster god gave me the chance to rewrite history so that I still had the papers—but would miss out on all that subsequently happened as a result of losing them—I'd decline the offer without a moment's hesitation. I don't mean to be overly Pollyanna-ish here; the one-off album cover gig was never going to be the salvation of my entire career—but it did make my life a hell of lot more interesting, and there are worse things than that.

Finally: the cartoons in this book cover a two year period beginning in the summer of 2008, with the presidential campaign in high gear and headed for the finish line. There are charmingly innocent cartoons in which I seem fully confident that the American people will recognize the extent to which Republicans were utterly wrong about everything. (Oh well.) There's the rise of the Tea Party, and of Crazy Glenn Beck, not to mention the Voices in His Head. There's the financial meltdown, the bailout and the stimulus, the now-discredited ACORN non-scandal (which still managed to destroy ACORN), and of course floating above it all, the Idea of Obama—the president a lot of people hoped they were voting for, as opposed to the one they got. (Not that anyone expected him to be a raging leftist, but did he really have to embrace so many Bush-era policies, from rendition to wiretapping, quite so enthusiastically?)

And as I noted at the outset, there's the crazy. The constant unending refrain, the low keening wail that just seems to grow louder every day: Obama's a Marxist, a fascist, a Muslim; progressives have a century-long plan devised by Woodrow Wilson to overthrow capitalism itself, blah blah blah *blah*—if you're paying the least little bit of attention, you've heard it all out there. In one of my cartoons from the late nineties, I suggested that when you scratch the surface you find that "everybody's nuts"—and I think we're about due for a sequel to that one. Actually this entire *book* probably serves as the follow-up to that cartoon. There was a time when we might have been able to at least politely pretend that most of the people around us had some tenuous connection to sanity, but thanks to chat boards and comments sections and Tea Party rallies and those aging standbys, talk radio and Fox News, we have all been thoroughly disabused of *that* notion. Now we know all too well just how much crazy there is around us at every moment.

Whether these cartoons add to the din or serve to counter it in some small way is left for the reader to decide.

Dan Perkins
(Tom Tomorrow)
New Haven, Connecticut
June 2010

THIS MODERN WORLD

by TOM TOMORROW

THE INSPIRATIONAL MEMOIR DEBUTED AT #1 ON THE NEW YORK TIMES BESTSELLER LIST.

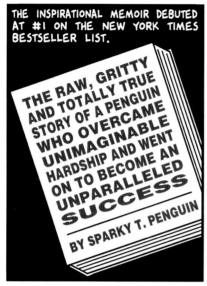

THE RAW, GRITTY AND TOTALLY TRUE STORY OF A PENGUIN WHO OVERCAME UNIMAGINABLE HARDSHIP AND WENT ON TO BECOME AN UNPARALLELED SUCCESS

BY SPARKY T. PENGUIN

THE AUTHOR WAS FEATURED ON EVERY MAJOR TALK SHOW.

YOU WERE A METH-SNORTING SEX ADDICT WITH AN INSURMOUNTABLE GAMBLING DEBT, FRAMED FOR A CRIME YOU DID NOT COMMIT! *HOW* DID YOU EVER MANAGE TO TURN YOUR LIFE AROUND?

WELL, OPRAH--I GUESS THE TURNING POINT CAME WHEN I WOKE UP IN AN ICE-FILLED BATHTUB WITH ONE OF MY *KIDNEYS* MISSING...

BUT THE MEDIA EXPOSURE PROVED TO BE HIS *UNDOING*...

HEY! I RECOGNIZE THAT PENGUIN, FROM THE NEWSPAPER I USE TO LINE THE BOTTOM OF THE BIRD CAGE!

...SOMETIMES YOU HAVE TO HIT ROCK BOTTOM, YOU KNOW?

YEAH--HE'S IN THAT CARTOON NO ONE READS!

HIS STORY QUICKLY UNRAVELLED!

IT TURNS OUT HE WAS *NOT* THE FIRST SELF-TAUGHT BRAIN SURGEON TO BECOME AN ASTRONAUT--AND PERFORM BRAIN SURGERY IN *SPACE*!

NOR IS HE A SELF-MADE BILLIONAIRE MARRIED TO THE WORLD'S MOST POPULAR LINGERIE MODEL!

I'M *UTTERLY* DISILLUSIONED!

THE PUBLISHER FACED EMBARAS-SING QUESTIONS FROM THE MEDIA.

SO--DO YOU PEOPLE BOTHER TO FACT CHECK THESE SO-CALLED MEMOIRS AT *ALL*?

SPARKY HAD AN HONEST FACE! IF HE SAID HE WAS RAISED BY FERAL WOLVES--WHO WERE *WE* TO DOUBT HIM?

BUT IN THE END, NO ONE WAS REALLY SURE WHAT EVER HAPPENED TO THE AUTHOR HIMSELF.

MAYBE HE WENT BACK TO THAT JOB HE HAD IN THAT CARTOON THAT NO ONE READS!

WHO WOULD EVER *KNOW*?

TOM TOMORROW©2009

1

THIS MODERN WORLD
by TOM TOMORROW

Panel 1: TONIGHT ON THE COMPLETELY BANAL NEWS NETWORK: WHO'S GOING TO WIN THE ELECTION, *OBAMA* OR *McCAIN*?

IT'LL CERTAINLY BE *ONE* OF THEM--UNLESS SOMETHING *UNEXPECTED* HAPPENS!

Panel 2: FOR INSTANCE, WHAT IF *HILLARY* JUMPS BACK INTO THE RACE AT THE LAST MINUTE?

IT COULD HAPPEN! OR MAYBE THERE WILL BE AN UNANTICIPATED NATIONWIDE SURGE OF SUPPORT FOR *BOB BARR*!

Panel 3: THE FUTURE IS CERTAINLY UNPREDICTABLE! HERE TO HELP US SORT IT ALL OUT IS OUR EXPERT ANALYST, THE *FORMER REPUBLICAN OPERATIVE*!

THANKS BIFF! IN *MY* EXPERT OPINION, *BARACK OBAMA'S* BEST MOVE AT THIS POINT WOULD BE TO SIMPLY *STOP CAMPAIGNING*!

Panel 4: EVERYONE'S GOING TO VOTE FOR HIM ANYWAY--SO WHY SHOULD HE WASTE ALL THAT TIME AND MONEY? IT'S SUMMERTIME! HE SHOULD *RELAX*! GO TO THE *BEACH*!

THANKS FOR THAT UNBIASED INSIGHT, FORMER REPUBLICAN OPERATIVE! NOW IT'S TIME FOR OUR BRIEF RUNDOWN OF *OTHER* NEWS!

Panel 5: TENS OF THOUSANDS OF PEOPLE DIE IN CATASTROPHIC WEATHER EVENT...HOUSING FORECLOSURES EVERYWHERE...PRICE OF GAS CONTINUES TO SKYROCKET...

BLAH BLAH BLAH, YADDA YADDA YADDA.

Panel 6: ALL RIGHT THEN! NOW THAT WE'VE GOT *THAT* OUT OF THE WAY, LET'S GET BACK TO *BUSINESS*!

ACCORDING TO THE LATEST POLLING DATA, OBAMA *COULD* WIN THE PRESIDENCY--UNLESS *McCAIN* DOES! WE'LL KEEP *SPECULATING*--AFTER *THESE MESSAGES*!

TOM TOMORROW©2008

THIS MODERN WORLD

by TOM TOMORROW

THE RISE AND (RELATIVE) FALL OF STUPIDITY IN AMERICA

AFTER 9/11, STUPIDITY BECAME PATRIOTIC.

BAD THING HAPPEN! US GO *KILL* PEOPLE NOW!

US SHOW WORLD WHO AM *BOSS!*

IT AM *ONLY THING TO DO!*

FOR SEVERAL YEARS, ANYONE WHO *QUESTIONED* STUPIDITY WAS INSULTED AND MALIGNED (THOUGH NOT VERY CLEVERLY, OF COURSE)...

YOU *DO* REALIZE THAT IRAQ HAD NOTHING TO DO WITH 9/11--?

YOU AM AMERICA-HATING TRAITOR WHO AM PROBABLY *HOMOSEXUAL!*

WHY YOU HATE BRAVE TROOPS?!

EVENTUALLY, HOWEVER, PEOPLE BEGAN TO NOTICE THAT STUPIDITY WASN'T WORKING OUT VERY WELL.

THE ECONOMY'S GONE TO HELL, THE CONSTITUTION'S BEEN SHREDDED, AND WE'RE APPARENTLY *NEVER* GETTING OUT OF IRAQ.

MAYBE LETTING STUPID PEOPLE RUN EVERYTHING *WASN'T* SUCH A GOOD IDEA.

AND NOW, AFTER SEVEN YEARS OF RELENTLESS STUPIDITY, NON-STUPID PEOPLE ARE FINALLY BEGINNING TO ASSERT THEIR NON-STUPIDITY--WITHIN REASONABLE *LIMITS*, OBVIOUSLY...

SHOULDN'T A PRESIDENT WHO AUTHORIZED *TORTURE* AND *ILLEGAL WIRETAPPING* BE SUBJECT TO--AH--

--MILD EXPRESSIONS OF DISAPPROVAL? AB-SOLUTELY!

OH--*RIGHT!* WE DON'T WANT TO GET *CARRIED AWAY!*

BUT SOONER OR LATER, STUPIDITY WILL STAGE A COMEBACK.

NEW BAD THING HAPPEN! US GO KILL *MORE* PEOPLE NOW!

AND US FURTHER DISREGARD BASIC PRINCIPLES WHICH ALLEGEDLY DEFINE US AS A PEOPLE!

IT AM *ONLY THING TO DO!*

TOM TOMORROW©2008

THIS MODERN WORLD

by TOM TOMORROW

THE ONGOING ADVENTURES OF **SPARKMAN** AND THE **BLINKSTER**

THIS WEEK: THEIR GREATEST **FOE!**

ON A PLEASANT AFTERNOON IN THE CITY, RESPONSIBLE CITIZENS DISCUSS THE **ISSUES**...

I HOPE THE WAR IS OVER BEFORE MY LITTLE SON IS GROWN!

I SYMPATHIZE COMPLETELY!

OH YES-- ME TOO!

THE CONVERSATION IS OVERHEARD BY RESPECTABLE NEW YORK TIMES COLUMNIST **WILLIAM KRISTOL**--

THAT YOUNG MOTHER'S ANTI-WAR DRIVEL IS WINNING THEM **OVER!**

--WHO IS ALSO--UNBEKNOWNST TO HIS EDITORS--

--THE SHAMELESS SUPERVILLAIN KNOWN AS...**THE PROPAGANDIST!**

MY **RECONTEXTUALIZATION BEAM** WILL TAKE CARE OF **HER!**

LLLLIEEEEZZZZ

URK! WHAT I MEAN TO SAY IS, I'M A **SELFISH ELITIST** WHO WANTS **OTHERS** TO BEAR THE BURDEN OF OUR VITAL STRUGGLE IN IRAQ!

ZZZZZ

WHY--I DO NOT SYMPATHIZE WITH YOU AT **ALL!**

NOR DO **I!**

FORTUNATELY OUR HEROES ARE ON PATROL NEARBY!

WHAT WAS THAT **NOISE**?

THAT WAS THE SOUND OF A **FALSE NARRATIVE** BEING IMPOSED--BY THAT FIENDISH MASTER OF **DECEIT**--

--THE **PROPAGANDIST!!**

QUICK, SPARKMAN! USE **YOUR** TRADEMARK WEAPON-- THE **HEAVY-HANDED RAY OF IRONIC JUSTICE!**

HAH! THAT WILL HAVE NO EFFECT ON **ME**, LITTLE DOGGIE! EVERYONE **KNOWS** THE SHAMELESS **PROPAGANDIST** IS IMMUNE TO **IRONY!**

NOW--PREPARE TO BE **KRIS-TOLIZED!**

LLLLIEEEEZZZZ

THE SMOKE CLEARS--AND THEN--

I...AM A... LATTE-SIPPING... **AMERICA-HATER!**

SNAP **OUT** OF IT, SPARKMAN!

BWAH HA HA HA!

CAN THIS REALLY BE...THE **END?** STAY **TUNED!**

TOM TOMORROW©2008

4

THIS MODERN WORLD

by TOM TOMORROW

5

THIS MODERN WORLD

by TOM TOMORROW

A FEW RECENT EXAMPLES OF AWESOMELY NON-RACIST POLITICAL DISCOURSE

WHEN TALK RADIO HOSTS DRAW PARALLELS BETWEEN THE MIDWESTERN FLOODS AND HURRICANE KATRINA--

YOU DIDN'T SEE *MIDWESTERNERS* WHINING FOR HELP, THE WAY THOSE PEOPLE IN *NEW ORLEANS* DID!

WHATEVER COLOR THEY WERE.

I DIDN'T EVEN *NOTICE!*

--THEY'RE SIMPLY MAKING AN INTERESTING *OBSERVATION*--WHICH HAS *NOTHING* TO DO WITH *RACE!*

WHEN FOX NEWS USES A SLANG TERM SYNONYMOUS WITH "UNWED MOTHER" IN REFERENCE TO MICHELLE OBAMA--

OBAMA'S BABY MAMA

--IT'S NOTHING MORE THAN A SLY POP CULTURAL *REFERENCE*--WITH *NO RACISM INVOLVED!*

WHEN FOX ANCHORS SPECULATE ABOUT THE POSSIBLE MEANING OF AN INNOCUOUS HAND GESTURE--

WAS IT A *TERRORIST FIST JAB?*

A *GANG SIGN?*

A SYMBOLIC REPRESENTATION OF THEIR *SECRET HATRED* FOR *WHITE PEOPLE?*

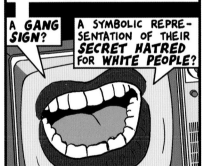

--THEY'RE ONLY DOING THEIR *JOBS* AS THOROUGH, RESPONSIBLE, NON-RACIST *JOURNALISTS!*

WHEN A VENDOR AT THE TEXAS GOP CONVENTION SELLS THESE BUTTONS ALL WEEKEND--

If Obama Is President... will we still call it The White House?

--WELL, IT'S JUST A HARMLESS POST-RACIAL JOKE AND *LIBERALS* ARE THE *REAL* RACISTS. OR, UM, SOMETHING.

NO DOUBT *ABOUT* IT--WE LIVE IN AN *AWESOMELY* COLORBLIND SOCIETY!

I BELIEVE WE SHOULD JUDGE OBAMA AND HIS WIFE BY THE *CONTENT* OF THEIR *CHARACTER!**

FOR INSTANCE-- DOES MICHELLE HATE "WHITEY" OR *NOT?*

AND WHAT'S UP WITH THAT *TERRORIST FIST JAB?*

INQUIRING NON-RACIST MINDS WANT TO *KNOW!*

*THE RIGHT'S FAVORITE M.L.K. QUOTE!

TOM TOMORROW©2008

THIS MODERN WORLD

OBAMA PHENOMENA

OBAMA DERANGEMENT SYNDROME: A PUZZLING MALADY WHICH CAUSES CRAZY PEOPLE TO BECOME *EVEN CRAZIER!*

I HEARD HE'S GOING TO COMMANDEER OUR *HOMES* AND GIVE THEM TO THE HORDES OF *ILLEGAL ALIENS* HE PLANS TO WELCOME ACROSS THE BORDER!

WELL IT MAKES *SENSE*, CONSIDERING THAT HE'S THE *ANTI-CHRIST* AND ALL!

UBIQUITIOUS APOSTATES: ON MESSAGE BOARDS ACROSS THE INTERNET, "FORMER DEMOCRATS" PROUDLY PROCLAIM THEIR NEWFOUND SUPPORT FOR *JOHN McCAIN!*

I am a lifelong Democrat--but I could NEVER vote for someone as inexperienced as Obama!
--Anonymous / 9:25 a.m.

As a disgruntled Hillary supporter, I couldn't agree MORE!
--Anonymous Too / 9:26 a.m.

HEH HEH!

TAP TAP TAP

DISILLUSIONED ACOLYTES: AS OBAMA'S POSITIONS ON ISSUES FROM ABORTION TO WARRANTLESS WIRETAPPING "EVOLVE", HIS MOST ARDENT SUPPORTERS FACE A *STUNNING* REALIZATION!

OUR PARTY'S PRESUMPTIVE PRESIDENTIAL NOMINEE IS BEHAVING LIKE--LIKE A *POLITICIAN!*

THESE ARE *NOT* THE OPINIONS HE EXPRESSED IN OUR MANY IMAGINARY CONVERSATIONS!

OBAMANOLOGISTS: TALMUDIC-LIKE SCHOLARS WHO STRIVE TO EXPLAIN THE DIFFERENCE BETWEEN WHAT OBAMA *SAYS* AND WHAT HE *MEANS!*

IT'S REALLY QUITE SIMPLE! ANYTHING HE SAYS THAT YOU *DISAGREE* WITH IS JUST *CAMPAIGN RHETORIC*--

--WHILE ANYTHING YOU *DO* AGREE WITH--IS A *HEARTFELT PROMISE!*

THE INVISIBLE CONSTITUENCY: THE UNSEEN, BUT APPARENTLY VITAL, DEMOGRAPHIC OBAMA HOPED TO WIN OVER BY VOTING TO EVISCERATE THE FOURTH AMENDMENT, IN KEEPING WITH THE BUSH ADMINISTRATION'S WISHES.

NO ONE HAS EVER OBSERVED THEM *DIRECTLY!* WE CAN ONLY *INFER* THEIR PRESENCE, AS A RESULT OF OBAMA'S FISA VOTE!

BECAUSE IF THEY *DON'T* EXIST, THERE'S NO RATIONAL EXPLANATION *FOR* THAT VOTE!

TOM TOMORROW©2008

THIS MODERN WORLD

by TOM TOMORROW

THIS WEEK: JUST A *FEW* OF THE REASONS REPUBLICANS EVERYWHERE ARE SIMPLY BRIMMING WITH...

MCCAIN MANIA!

1. JOHN McCAIN REPRESENTS THE *FUTURE!* WHY--HE HAS EVEN PROMISED TO FAMILIARIZE HIMSELF WITH THE *INTERNET* SOON!

SO THIS IS YOUR *COMPUTING MACHINE,* EH?

SO WHERE ARE THE *PUNCHCARDS* AND *FLASHING LIGHTS*?

WILL IT *EXPLODE* IF SOMETHING I SAY *"DOES NOT COMPUTE"*?

2. HE HAS A *VERY SERIOUS PLAN* TO SOLVE OUR NATION'S ILLS!

SO MY FRIENDS, AFTER WE WIN THE WAR IN IRAQ WE'LL HAVE ENOUGH MONEY LEFT OVER TO BALANCE THE *BUDGET--*

--AND IF WE HAVE A BALANCED BUDGET, THAT'LL GIVE US MORE RESOURCES TO WIN THE WAR IN *IRAQ*!

WHOOPS! I'M DOING THAT CREEPY-SMILE-FACE THING AGAIN, AREN'T I?

3. HE IS IN TOUCH WITH THE CONCERNS OF *ORDINARY CITIZENS*--AND SO ARE HIS *ADVISERS*!

"THIS IS A *MENTAL RECESSION!*"

"WE HAVE BECOME A NATION OF *WHINERS!*"

ECONOMIC ADVISER PHIL "LOST MONEY INVESTING IN SEXPLOITATION MOVIES" GRAMM

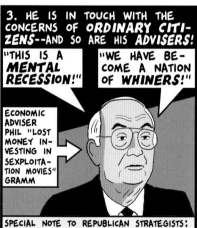

SPECIAL NOTE TO REPUBLICAN STRATEGISTS: GRAMM'S INEXPLICABLE RESIGNATION FROM THE McCAIN CAMPAIGN NOTWITHSTANDING, INSULTING VOTERS IS A *SUREFIRE PATH* TO *VICTORY*--AND DON'T LET *ANYONE* TELL YOU *OTHERWISE*!

4. HE HAS A *CHARMING* PENCHANT FOR OFF-THE-CUFF *HUMOR*--LIKE HIS RECENT JOKE ABOUT CIGARETTE EXPORTS BEING A GOOD WAY TO *KILL IRANIAN CIVILIANS*!

HEH HEH! THAT'S RIGHT! AND YOU WANT TO KNOW *ANOTHER* GOOD WAY TO KILL THEM?

BOMBS.

5. FINALLY, WE CAN'T FORGET THE MAVERICKY *STRAIGHT TALK* FOR WHICH HE IS SO WIDELY RENOWNED!

YOU'VE ADMITTED THAT YOU'RE NOT AN ECONOMIC EXPERT--

NO I HAVEN'T.

ER--YES, YOU HAVE. WE HAVE IT ON TAPE.

WHAT? YOU MEAN YOU HAVE SOME METHOD OF *RECORDING* THE WORDS I SPEAK?

WHY DIDN'T ANYONE *TELL* ME ABOUT THIS?!

TOM TOMORROW©2008

9

THIS MODERN WORLD

by TOM TOMORROW

THIS MODERN WORLD

by TOM TOMORROW

SPARKY T. PENGUIN, PRIVATE EYE...IN

FAREWELL, MY LOVELY ECONOMY

HELLO! I'M THE *INVISIBLE HAND* OF THE *FREE MARKET!*

SO HOW COME I CAN *SEE* YOU?

UH--MAGIC OF THE MARKET-PLACE. JUST GO WITH IT.

LOOK, I NEED YOUR *HELP!* TWO YEARS AGO, I WAS RIDING *HIGH!* HOUSING PRICES WERE *SOARING!* BANKS WERE HANDING OUT LOANS TO ANYONE WHO *ASKED*--AND THEN SELLING THE DEBT TO *INVESTORS!* AS LONG AS PEOPLE KEPT *BORROWING MONEY,* EVERYTHING WORKED *GREAT!*

BUT *NOW,* IT SUDDENLY TURNS OUT THAT THERE'S A MOUNTAIN OF *BAD DEBT* OUT THERE! MORTGAGE LENDERS ARE COLLAPSING ALL *OVER* THE PLACE! I DON'T UNDERSTAND HOW ANY OF THIS COULD HAVE *POSSIBLY* HAPPENED--BUT IT'S MAKING ME *VERY TWITCHY!*

I'M SURE IT IS--

--BUT *I* CAN'T HELP YOU! YOU'RE A *JUNKIE*--STRUNG OUT ON THE EVER-INCREASING LEVELS OF *DEBT* AMERICANS HAD TO INCUR FOR YOU TO MAINTAIN YOUR *ECONOMIC HIGH!* YOU BLED YOUR SOURCES *DRY*--AND NOW YOU'RE SUFFERING FROM *WITHDRAWAL!*

YOU DON'T NEED A PRIVATE EYE-- YOU NEED A STINT IN *REHAB!*

STOP IT! THAT'S *CRAZY TALK!* THE INVISIBLE HAND OF THE FREE MARKET IS *NOT* ADDICTED TO SOCIETALLY UNSUSTAINABLE LEVELS OF *DEBT!* THAT WOULD NOT BE *RATIONAL!*

I CAN QUIT ANY TIME I *WANT!*

I JUST DON'T *WANT*--

YO, *HAND!*

I'VE BEEN LOOKIN' FOR YOU *EVERYWHERE!* HOW DOES A $25 BILLION *BAILOUT* SOUND TO YOU?

LIKE THE FIX I *NEED*--AT LEAST, UNTIL THE *NEXT* ONE!

ALL RIGHT, THEN! FORGET *THIS* LOSER--LET'S GO *SCORE!*

AS HE LEFT, I WONDERED HOW LONG IT WOULD TAKE HIM TO HIT *ROCK BOTTOM*--AND HOW BIG A MESS HE WAS GONNA MAKE WHEN HE *DID...*

TOM TOMORROW©2008

THIS MODERN WORLD

by TOM TOMORROW

ALWAYS GOOD FOR McCAIN

THE DEMOCRATIC CONVENTION WAS GOOD FOR McCAIN.

ONLY A *CELEBRITY* COULD FILL A FOOTBALL STADIUM LIKE THAT--AND IF THERE'S ONE THING AMERICANS CAN'T STAND, IT'S *CELEBRITIES!*

THE REPUBLICAN CONVENTION WAS GOOD FOR McCAIN.

COMPARED TO SOME OF THOSE DELEGATES, JOHN McCAIN LOOKED POSITIVE-LY *YOUTHFUL!*

GEORGE BUSH'S POLL NUMBERS ARE GOOD FOR McCAIN.

VOTERS ARE HUNGRY FOR *CHANGE*--THAT ONLY A MAVERICK LIKE *JOHN McCAIN* CAN PROVIDE!

BARACK OBAMA'S POLL NUMBERS ARE GOOD FOR McCAIN.

CONSIDERING WHAT A MESS REPUBLICANS HAVE MADE OF THINGS, OBAMA *SHOULD* HAVE A MUCH *GREATER* LEAD!

THE QUESTION OF BARACK OBAMA'S EXPERIENCE IS GOOD FOR McCAIN.

FOUR YEARS IN THE U.S. SENATE ISN'T ENOUGH TIME TO LEARN ANYTHING ABOUT *LEADERSHIP!*

THE QUESTION OF SARAH PALIN'S EXPERIENCE IS GOOD FOR McCAIN.

ONE AND A HALF YEARS AS GOVERNOR OF ALASKA IS *PLENTY* OF TIME TO LEARN ABOUT LEAD-ERSHIP!

PALIN'S TIES TO ALASKAN SECESSIONISTS ARE GOOD FOR McCAIN.

AMERICANS CAN *RELATE* TO HER HATRED OF THE GOVERNMENT SHE WILL BE AN ELDERLY MAN'S HEARTBEAT AWAY FROM LEADING!

PALIN'S PREGNANT TEEN-AGE DAUGHTER IS GOOD FOR McCAIN.

AMERICANS CAN *TOTALLY* RELATE TO THE MESSY REALITIES OF LIFE WHICH REPUBLICAN POLICIES RARELY ACKNOWLEDGE!

HIS OPPOSITION TO OFF-SHORE DRILLING WAS GOOD FOR McCAIN.

AS A FORMER P.O.W., HE HAS THE *CHARACTER* TO DO WHAT IS RIGHT!

HIS NEWFOUND SUPPORT FOR OFFSHORE DRILLLING IS GOOD FOR McCAIN.

AS A FORMER P.O.W., HE HAS THE *COURAGE* TO DO WHAT IS NECESSARY!

IF OUR ENTIRE PLANET IS DESTROYED BY A BY A ROGUE ASTEROID NEXT MONTH, IT WILL BE GOOD FOR McCAIN.

AT LEAST THEN, HE WOULD NOT HAVE TO RISK EN-DURING A HUMILIATING DEFEAT IN *NOVEMBER!*

THIS MODERN WORLD

by TOM TOMORROW

THE McCAIN CAMPAIGN MOCKS OBAMA'S RHETORIC.

ENOUGH WITH THE *HOPE*, ALREADY!

OUR CANDIDATE BELIEVES IN THE AUDACITY OF *BLEAK DESPAIR!*

McCAIN '08 — HE'LL GET THOSE KIDS OFF YOUR LAWN

THEY MOCK HIS POPULARITY.

YOU KNOW WHO *ELSE* DREW GIANT CROWDS IN GERMANY? *ADOLF HITLER,* THAT'S WHO!

JUST SAYIN'.

McCAIN '08 — HE'LL GET THOSE KIDS OFF YOUR LAWN

THEY MOCK HIS PHYSICAL FITNESS.

SO SENATOR FANCY PANTS "EXERCISES" AND "EATS RIGHT"! BIG *DEAL!*

VOTERS WANT A PRESIDENT WHO *LOOKS* LIKE AMERICA *FEELS* RIGHT NOW-- *DECREPIT* AND *WORN OUT!*

'08 SE KIDS LAWN

THEY MOCK HIM FOR STATING THE OBVIOUS.

OBAMA THINKS WE SHOULD INFLATE OUR *TIRES* FOR BETTER *GAS MILEAGE!*

HA HA! AND I SUPPOSE HE THINKS *BRUSHING* HELPS FIGHT *CAVITIES!*

M — HE'LL GET TH E KIDS OFF YOUR LAWN

THEY MOCK HIS ALLEGED MESSIANIC TENDENCIES.

LISTEN TO THIS! OBAMA SAYS "I FEEL LIKE *GOD* WANTS ME TO RUN FOR PRESIDENT!" IS HE PRESUMPTUOUS OR *WHAT?*

UH--ACTUALLY THAT'S SOMETHING GEORGE W. BUSH ONCE SAID.

OH! WELL, THE PRESIDENT *IS* A MAN OF *FAITH!*

HE'LL G TH OFF YOUR LA N

THEY MOCK HIM FOR NOT VISITING WOUNDED TROOPS--

HE THINKS HE'S TOO *IMPORTANT* TO WASTE TIME VISITING WITH OUR BRAVE FALLEN HEROES! IT IS AN *OUTRAGE!*

--WITH A BACKUP PLAN TO MOCK HIM IF HE *DOES.* *

HE THINKS HE'S SO IMPORTANT, HE CAN USE OUR BRAVE FALLEN HEROES AS A *BACKDROP* IN HIS *PHOTO OP!* IT IS AN *OUTRAGE!*

*TRUE!

BUT MOSTLY, THEY MOCK THEIR *OWN* CANDIDATE'S PROMISE TO RUN A CLEAN CAMPAIGN AND STICK TO THE ISSUES.

--AND WE MUST DO THESE THINGS--*BUT*--

DID HE JUST SAY "*BUTT*"? LIKE HE THINKS *HIS* DOESN'T *STINK?*

OR THE TROOPS' DO?

SOUNDS LIKE A GAFFE TO *ME!*

M HE'LL OFF Y UR LA

TOM TOMORROW©2008

13

THIS MODERN WORLD

by TOM TOMORROW

Panel 1:
OVER THE YEARS, ORDINARY CITIZENS BECAME INCREASINGLY INVESTED IN THE MARKET.

WHAT *ELSE* ARE YOU GONNA DO WITH YOUR MONEY? LEAVE IT SITTING IN SOME LOW-INTEREST *BANK ACCOUNT*?

THE MARKET *ALWAYS* PAYS OFF IN THE *LONG RUN*!

TRUST US!

Panel 2:

MEANWHILE, INVESTMENT BANKERS WERE BUSY CREATING FINANCIAL INSTRUMENTS TOO CONVOLUTED FOR THE HUMAN MIND TO COMPREHEND.

WE JUST KEEP SLICING AND RECONFIGURING ALL THESE *BAD HOUSING LOANS*--

--AND SOMEHOW WE JUST KEEP GETTING *RICHER*!

Panel 3:
UNSURPRISINGLY, THIS WASN'T A VERY GOOD IDEA.

OH MY GOD! OUR PORTFOLIO OF *WORTHLESS HOUSING DEBT*... TURNS OUT TO BE *WORTHLESS*!

WHO COULD HAVE *EVER* SEEN THIS COMING?

Panel 4:

OF COURSE, THE GENIUSES WHO CREATED THIS MESS ARE EFFECTIVELY HOLDING OUR ENTIRE ECONOMY *HOSTAGE*.

IF *WE* GO DOWN, WE'RE TAKING THE REST OF YOU *WITH* US!

WE'RE *TOO BIG TO FAIL*, SUCKERS!

Panel 5:

THE ADMINISTRATION WANTS TO *REWARD* THEIR MISTAKES BY RAMMING THROUGH AN ENORMOUS BAILOUT WITH LITTLE OVERSIGHT.

WHAT A RELIEF! THE WISDOM OF THE MARKETPLACE HAS GIVEN US A *RATIONAL SOLUTION*--

--DUMP THE WHOLE STINKING PILE ON THE *TAXPAYERS*!

Panel 6:

AND GOSH, GIVING THE BUSH ADMINISTRATION THE BENEFIT OF THE DOUBT HAS ALWAYS WORKED OUT SO WELL IN THE PAST.

NO TIME TO *THINK*! NO TIME FOR *QUESTIONS*! IF CONGRESS DOESN'T APPROVE THIS BAILOUT *IMMEDIATELY*, YOU'RE GONNA SPEND YOUR RETIREMENT EATING *CAT FOOD*!

WE'RE ALL IN THIS *TOGETHER*, RIGHT BUCKO?

JUST--SOME OF US MORE THAN *OTHERS*!

THIS MODERN WORLD

by TOM TOMORROW

ON *PARALLEL EARTH* (WHERE EVENTS BEAR *NO RELATIONSHIP* TO THOSE HERE AT HOME), THE REPUBLICAN PRESIDENTIAL CANDIDATE IS AN *ACTUAL NEANDERTHAL.*

UGG MIGHTY *HUNTER!* UGG SMASH ENEMIES WITH *BIG ROCKS!*

BUT WHAT WILL YOU DO ABOUT THE *ECONOMIC* CRISIS?

UM--SMASH SOMEBODY WITH *BIG ROCK*, OF COURSE!

SOME PARALLEL CITIZENS HARBOR DOUBTS ABOUT HIS LEADERSHIP STYLE.

HIS ECONOMIC APPROACH IS A LITTLE *HEAVY HANDED*, IF YOU ASK *ME!*

I WORRY THAT HE REPRE-SENTS A RETURN TO THE POLITICS OF THE *PAST!*

AND HIS CHOICE OF A RUNNING MATE CAUGHT MOST OBSERVERS OFF GUARD.

LADIES AND GENTLEMEN, THE NEXT VICE PRESIDENT OF THE UNITED STATES--A *DEER CAUGHT IN THE HEADLIGHTS!*

I'M EXTREMELY PREPARED TO LEAD THIS COUNTRY.

PARALLEL DEMOCRATS INITIALLY THOUGHT THE UGG CAMPAIGN HAD MADE A HUGE STRATEGIC BLUNDER.

SURELY NO ONE WILL VOTE TO PUT A DEER CAUGHT IN THE HEAD-LIGHTS A HEARTBEAT AWAY FROM THE *PRESIDENCY!*

ESPECIALLY CONSIDERING THE *BREVITY* OF THE AVERAGE NEANDERTHAL *LIFESPAN!*

BUT THE NOMINEE TURNED OUT TO BE ENORMOUSLY POPULAR WITH THE PARALLEL CONSERVATIVE BASE.

HER SMUG YET UNCOMPREHENDING GAZE REFLECTS THE BEWILDER-MENT *WE* FEEL--

--AS WE STARE INTO THE ONRUSHING HEADLIGHTS OF *GODLESS LIBERAL ELITISM!*

AND HER MEDIA APPEARANCES WENT...ABOUT AS WELL AS YOU'D EXPECT, ACTUALLY...

SO WHAT CAN YOU TELL US ABOUT YOUR *FOREIGN POLICY* EXPERIENCE?

YIKES! SHE LOOKS LIKE--UM--LIKE--

--OH, IF *ONLY I* COULD THINK OF AN APPROPRIATE *SIMILE!*

TOM TOMORROW©2008... www.thismodernworld.com

16

THIS MODERN WORLD

by TOM TOMORROW

WHEN ALL ELSE FAILS, REPUBLICANS CAN ALWAYS RELY ON...

THE POLITICS OF RESENTMENT

GRANTED, THEIR DENUNCIATIONS OF BIG CITY ELITISTS ARE OFTEN LESS THAN *CREDIBLE*...

CAN YOU *BELIEVE* THESE EAST COAST WACKOS AND THEIR "COSMOPOLITAN" VALUES? SNICKER!

THEY'RE CERTAINLY NOT REGULAR FOLKS LIKE YOU AND *ME!*

RUDY THE CROSS-DRESSING MAYOR

BUT SOMETIMES THEY FIND A MORE PLAUSIBLE STANDARD-BEARER.

SO BARACK OBAMA THINKS WE'RE *IGNORANT*--JUST BECAUSE WE DON'T BELIEVE IN *BIRTH CONTROL*, OR *SCIENCE*, OR ANY OF THAT STUFF!

IS THAT GUY A *KNOW-IT-ALL* OR *WHAT*?

McCAIN FOR PRESIDENT

PALIN FOR PRESIDENT-AS-SOON-AS-McCAIN-CROAKS

YOU HAVE TO WONDER IF THE STRATEGY WOULD BE AS SUCCESSFUL--IF ITS TARGETS WEREN'T SO EAGER TO PLAY ALONG...

IF DEMOCRATS WANT TO WIN, WE MUST SHOW THAT WE, TOO, EMBRACE THE MYTHICAL VALUES OF SMALL TOWN AMERICA AS DEFINED BY REPUBLICANS!

I WISH WE WERE IN SUCH A TOWN RIGHT *NOW!*

WE COULD GO TO A *COUNTY FAIR* OR SOMETHING!

BLAME IT ON THE ELECTORAL COLLEGE...IF PRESIDENTS WERE ELECTED BY POPULAR VOTE, WE'D HAVE AN ENTIRELY DIFFERENT GAME...

REMEMBER THE *OLD* DAYS--WHEN THE CONCERNS OF A SMALL MINORITY OF SOCIALLY CONSERVATIVE SWING STATE VOTERS COMPLETELY DOMINATED OUR POLITICAL DISCOURSE?

WHAT COULD WE POSSIBLY HAVE BEEN *THINKING*?

IN THE MEANTIME, IT'S PRETTY CLEAR WHICH PARTY *ACTUALLY* VIEWS AVERAGE AMERICANS WITH CONTEMPT...

YOU THINK VOTERS ARE *REALLY* GONNA FALL FOR ALL THIS *RESENTMENT* CRAP?

SURE! LIKE PHIL GRAMM SAYS, THEY'RE ALL A BUNCH OF *WHINERS!*

ANYWAY, WHAT ELSE HAVE WE GOT?

TOM TOMORROW©2008... www.thismodernworld.com

THIS MODERN WORLD

by TOM TOMORROW

THIS WEEK: A FEW OF JOHN McCAIN AND SARAH PALIN'S 100% GENUINE AND EXTREMELY COMPELLING REASONS TO VOTE FOR JOHN McCAIN AND SARAH PALIN

OBAMA IS *INEXPERIENCED!*

HE HAS CERTAINLY NEVER HAD TO KEEP AN EYE ON PUTIN REARING HIS HEAD AND COMING INTO THE AIR SPACE OF THE UNITED STATES OF AMERICA AND, UM, STUFF LIKE THAT!

DID I MENTION THAT I AM *VERY, VERY HEALTHY*, MY FRIENDS?

BLINK BLINK BLINK

JOE BIDEN IS AN ELDERLY POLITICAL *INSIDER!*

HE'S BEEN IN WASHINGTON SINCE I WAS, LIKE, IN SECOND GRADE! HE REPRESENTS THE *STATUS QUO*--AND *WE* REPRESENT YOUTH-FUL *ENERGY* AND, LIKE, *CHANGE!*

THAT'S RIGHT, MY FRIENDS! WHAT THE *YOUNGSTER* SAID!

WINK!

JOHN McCAIN IS THE *REAL* REFORMER!

IF BY "REFORMER" YOU MEAN SOME-ONE WHO HAS LONG DESCRIBED HIM-SELF AS AN *OPPONENT* OF MOST GOVERNMENT REGULATION! BUT ONLY NIXON CAN GO TO CHINA, RIGHT, MY FRIENDS?

ONLY *WHO* CAN GO *WHERE*?

BLINK BLINK BLINK

THE OBAMA CAMPAIGN IS ALWAYS LOOKING *BACKWARDS!*

THEY KEEP BRINGING UP THE *BUSH* ADMINISTRATION AND STUFF! I MEAN, THAT'S, LIKE, *ANCIENT HISTORY*, DON'TCHA KNOW!

WHY WON'T THEY ADDRESS THE *TIMELY* ISSUES, MY FRIENDS--SUCH AS THE *WEATHER UNDERGROUND*?

WINK!

AND OF COURSE--OBAMA IS *ERRATIC!*

JOE THE PLUMBER DOESN'T NEED *THAT*, MY FRIENDS! JOE THE PLUMB-ER NEEDS THE STEADFAST LEADER-SHIP *I* HAVE EXHIBITED *THROUGH-OUT* THIS CAMPAIGN! JOE THE PLUMBER DESERVES NO *LESS!*

AND IF *THAT* DOESN'T WORK FOR YA--*I'LL* BE BACK IN 2012!

WHAT?

WHAT?

BLINK BLINK BLINK

TOM TOMORROW©2008... www.thismodernworld.com

18

THIS MODERN WORLD

by TOM TOMORROW

Panel 1:

TONIGHT WE'LL BE DISCUSSING THE LATEST *STUPID CAMPAIGN SEASON DISTRACTION* THAT WE IN THE MEDIA KEEP TALKING ABOUT!

WHY *IS* THE STUPID DISTRACTION GETTING SO MUCH ATTENTION, RATHER THAN ALL THE SUBSTANTIVE ISSUES WE *AREN'T* TALKING ABOUT?

Panel 2:

SOME HAVE SUGGESTED THAT WE IN THE MEDIA MAY ACTUALLY BEAR SOME *RESPONSIBILITY* FOR THE EXCESSIVE ATTENTION BEING PAID TO THE STUPID DISTRACTION--BUT THIS IS, OF COURSE, ABSURD!

INDEED IT *IS*, WANDA!

Panel 3:

AFTER ALL--THE MEDIA DID NOT *CREATE* THE STUPID DISTRACTION! WE'VE SIMPLY REPORTED THE *FACTS*-- AND PROVIDED ENDLESS HOURS OF *ANALYSIS* AND *COMMENTARY*!

THAT'S *TRUE*, BIFF! WE'RE NOT RESPONSIBLE FOR THE PERCEIVED *IMPORTANCE* OF THE STUPID DISTRACTION--

Panel 4:

--BUT IF THE STUPID DISTRACTION *IS* PERCEIVED AS IMPORTANT, WE HAVE NO CHOICE BUT TO DISCUSS IT *FURTHER*!

THE ENTIRE PROCESS IS *COMPLETELY* OUT OF OUR *CONTROL*! WE HAVE *NOTHING* TO DO WITH *ANY* OF IT!

Panel 5:

WHY--*I* CAN'T EVEN REMEMBER HOW I GOT TO THE STUDIO THIS MORNING! IT'S AS IF MY BODY SIMPLY *BROUGHT* ME HERE OF ITS *OWN VOLITION*!

WHY DO MY LIPS KEEP FLAPPING AND MAKING THESE *NOISES*?

PLEASE STOP US-- BEFORE WE WASTE ANY *MORE* TIME ON THE STUPID DISTRACTION--

Panel 6:

--*WHICH* OUR ROUNDTABLE OF EXPERTS WILL EXAMINE *IN DEPTH* IN JUST ONE MOMENT!

AND: IS THE STUPID DISTRACTION NOTHING MORE THAN A *STUPID DISTRACTION*? WE'LL SEE WHAT RANDOM PEOPLE ON THE STREET THINK!

ALL THAT AND *MORE* ABOUT THE YOU-KNOW-WHAT...AFTER THESE MESSAGES.

TOM TOMORROW©2008

THIS MODERN WORLD

by TOM TOMORROW

SO SARAH PALIN HAS BEEN MOCK-ING OBAMA'S COMMENT ABOUT U.S. TROOPS IN AFGHANISTAN 'AIR-RAID-ING VILLAGES AND KILLING CIVIL-IANS'...SHE SAYS IT'S NOT TRUE, AND HER INCREASINGLY NASTY AUDIENCES HAVE BEEN CALLING OBAMA A TRAITOR, AND **WORSE**...

WELL IF THE SHOE *FITS*...

FUNNY THING IS, *U.S. MILITARY INVESTIGATORS* HAVE JUST CONCLUDED THAT AT LEAST THIRTY AFGHAN CIVILIANS WERE KILLED IN AN *AIR RAID* OF THEIR VILLAGE, LAST AUGUST...

AND NOT ONLY **THAT**--DEFENSE SECRETARY ROBERT GATES RECENTLY **APOLOGIZED** TO AFGHANS FOR THE "LOSS OF INNOCENT LIFE AS A RE-SULT OF COALITION AIRSTRIKES."

WHOEVER PUT THOSE WORDS IN SARAH PALIN'S MOUTH IS SIMPLY **LYING**. AND THEY'RE BANKING ON YOU BEING TOO STUPID AND IGNORANT TO GOOGLE IT FOR **YOURSELF**.

WITH THE ECONOMY COLLAPSING AND CONSERVATISM IN A SHAMBLES, THEY'VE GOT NOTHING **LEFT** BUT THE POLITICS OF INNUENDO AND FEAR--IMPLYING THAT OBAMA HATES THE TROOPS, THAT HE'S STRANGE AND DIFFERENT, THAT HE CAN'T BE **TRUSTED**!

COME ON, BIFF--SURELY EVEN *YOU* CAN SEE THROUGH *THAT*!

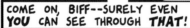

I HEARD HE'S BEST FRIENDS WITH THAT **TERRORIST** GUY.

GOSH, IT'S GOING TO BE A LONG THREE WEEKS, ISN'T IT.

TOM TOMORROW©2008...www.thismodernworld.com

THIS MODERN WORLD

by TOM TOMORROW

ONCE AGAIN, IT'S TIME TO ASK...
ARE YOU A *REAL* AMERICAN?

ARE YOU AMONG THE **TWENTY PERCENT** OF AMERICANS WHO LIVE IN RURAL AREAS AND SMALL TOWNS?*

YOU JUST CAN'T **TRUST** THOSE DECADENT ELITISTS WHO LIVE IN OR AROUND **CITIES!**

NOT TO **MENTION** THE NORTHEAST, THE UPPER MIDWEST, THE WEST COAST, AND VARIOUS POCKETS OF THE **SOUTH!**

*ACCORDING TO 2000 U.S. CENSUS DATA.

DO YOU AGREE WITH RECENT MCCAIN RALLY ATTENDEES THAT SENATOR OBAMA IS A COMMUNIST, A TERRORIST, AND/OR A TRAITOR, BEST REPRESENTED BY SMALL **MONKEY DOLLS?**

THIS IS **LITTLE HUSSEIN!**

HEH HEH HEH HEH HEH!*

*ACTUAL MCCAIN SUPPORTER, AS SEEN ON YOU TUBE.

ARE YOU UTTERLY OBLIVIOUS TO THE DISTINCTION BETWEEN VOTER **REGISTRATION** FRAUD AND ACTUAL **VOTE FRAUD?**

IF SOMEONE SUBMITS A FALSE **REGISTRATION** IN THE NAME OF **MICKEY MOUSE--**

--OUR ENTIRE **DEMOCRACY** IS IMPERILED!

IN SOME UNSPECIFIED MANNER THAT I DON'T ENTIRELY UNDERSTAND.

DO YOU BELIEVE THAT THE SUBPRIME MELTDOWN CAN BE BLAMED ON THE 1977 **COMMUNITY REINVESTMENT ACT,** ALL EVIDENCE TO THE **CONTRARY?***

DETAILS, SCHMEETAILS! ALL **I** KNOW IS, THIS LETS US PIN THE WHOLE MESS ON **DEMOCRATS** AND **BLACK PEOPLE!**

MY **FAVORITE** SCAPEGOATS!

*THE MAJORITY OF BAD SUBPRIME LOANS WERE ISSUED BY INSTITUTIONS NOT COVERED UNDER THE ACT.

AND--DO YOU OPPOSE A TAX INCREASE FOR UPPER INCOME AMERICANS WHILE SIMULTANEOUSLY SUPPORTING THE WAR IN IRAQ, WHICH IS COSTING US $10 BILLION A **MONTH?**

OF COURSE! **I'D** LIKE TO BE RICH SOME DAY--AND I **CERTAINLY** WOULDN'T WANT MY HYPOTHETICAL SUCCESS TO BE PUNISHED WITH **HIGHER TAXES!**

OH, AND GOD BLESS THE TROOPS.

IF YOU ANSWERED "YES" TO ALL THESE QUESTIONS--CONGRATULATIONS! YOU **MIGHT** BE PART OF THAT ELITE, EVER-DIMINISHING SEGMENT OF THE POPULATION KNOWN TO RIGHT-WING IDEOLOGUES AS "**REAL**" AMERICANS!

BUT **WAIT**--IF WE'RE PART OF AN "ELITE" GROUP--DOESN'T THAT MAKE US...**ELITISTS?**

IN WHICH CASE--**WE** MUST HATE AMERICA **TOO!**

I **DENOUNCE** US!

TOM TOMORROW©2008... www.thismodernworld.com

21

THIS MODERN WORLD

Panel 1:
GOOD EVENING AND WELCOME TO THE ACTION MCNEWS NETWORK! TONIGHT WE'LL BE TAKING A LOOK AT THE INCREDIBLE STORY OF...

JOHN McCAIN'S LAST MINUTE PATH TO VICTORY!

Panel 2:
IT ALL BEGAN A WEEK BEFORE THE ELECTION, WITH THE ADVICE OF TWO PROMINENT COLUMNISTS!

LOOK AT *THIS*! KRISTOL SAYS WE SHOULD MENTION THE *SURGE* MORE OFTEN--AND DICK MORRIS SAYS WE NEED TO CALL OBAMA A *SOCIALIST*!

OF *COURSE*! WHY DIDN'T WE THINK OF THESE THINGS *SOONER*?

Panel 3:
AS A REINVIGORATED MCCAIN HIT THE CAMPAIGN TRAIL, AN ASTONISHING TRANSFORMATION BEGAN!

I *WAS* GOING TO VOTE FOR OBAMA-- UNTIL I HEARD ABOUT HIM BEING A *SOCIALIST* AND ALL!

I DID NOT REALIZE THAT JOHN MCCAIN SUPPORTED THE *SURGE*! HE'S SURE GOT MY VOTE *NOW*!

Panel 4:
EQUALLY STUNNING WAS THE SWIFT TURNAROUND IN PUBLIC OPINION REGARDING *SARAH PALIN*!

I *USED* TO THINK SHE WAS A *NITWIT*--BUT NOW I REALIZE THAT HER MOUTH SIMPLY CAN'T KEEP UP WITH HER *BIG BRAIN*!

IT'S WHY SHE WEARS HER HAIR LIKE THAT, YOU KNOW-- TO COVER THE BULGE OF HER *OVERSIZED CRANIUM*!

Panel 5:
ON NOVEMBER 4, EVERY LEADING POLL GAVE MCCAIN AN INSUR- MOUNTABLE LEAD.

--AND THERE IS *NO POSSIBLE WAY* THAT BARACK OBAMA CAN WIN THIS ELECTION *NOW*!

WHAT A *LOSER*! AND TO IMAGINE THAT JUST A FEW SCANT DAYS AGO, WE HAD ALL BUT *CORONATED* HIM!

I HOPE SEN- ATOR MCCAIN CAN FIND IT IN HIS HEART TO *FORGIVE* US!

Panel 6:
AND THEN JOHN MCCAIN WOKE UP.

ZZZZZZzz--SNORT--HUH--WHAT? OH...MUSTA DOZED OFF...

IS IT TIME FOR MY *VICTORY PARTY* YET?!

BLINK BLINK BLINK

www.thismodernworld.com

TOM TOMORROW©2008...

22

THIS MODERN WORLD

by TOM TOMORROW

I CAN'T *UNDERSTAND* IT! DESPITE *CLEAR* WARNINGS THAT OBAMA IS A *SOCIALIST*--

--AND DESPITE THE EFFORTS OF INTREPID *INTERNET DETECTIVES* WHO HAVE DEMONSTRATED THAT OBAMA'S BIRTH CERTIFICATE IS A *FAKE* AND THAT HIS REAL FATHER WAS VERY PROBABLY *MALCOLM X*--

--AMERICANS ELECTED HIM *ANYWAY!* IT'S AS IF THE ENTIRE COUNTRY HAS GONE *MAD!*

WELL? DON'T YOU HAVE SOME WILDLY IMPLAUSIBLE LEFT WING REJOINDER? SOMETHING ABOUT THE ALLEGED FAILURES OF THE *BUSH ADMINISTRATION*, OR CONSERVATISM *ITSELF*? OR MAYBE SOMETHING SNARKY ABOUT *SARAH PALIN'S* QUALIFICATIONS?

NAH. I JUST WANT TO SAVOR THIS MOMENT A LITTLE WHILE LONGER.

BECAUSE OBAMA WASN'T RUNNING AGAINST GEORGE BUSH! AND GEORGE BUSH ISN'T *REALLY* A CONSERVATIVE! AND THE MEDIA WERE IN THE *TANK* FOR OBAMA! AND JOE THE PLUMBER IS A *REAL* AMERICAN BLAH B BLAH *BLAH* BLA B BLA BLA BL B

TOM TOMORROW©2008... www.thismodernworld.com

23

24

THIS MODERN WORLD

by TOM TOMORROW

Panel 1: RIGHT-WING BLOGGERS...TALK RADIO HOSTS...FOX NEWS...

THEY TRIED TO WARN US

IF ONLY WE'D *LISTENED*-- WHILE THERE WAS *STILL* TIME!

WHAT *FOOLS* WE WERE!

Panel 2: SURE, HE PLAYED IT REAL COOL AFTER THE ELECTION.

AND I, UH, BELIEVE WE NEED TO, UH, PURSUE A BIPARTISAN, UH, APPROACH TO SOLVING OUR NATION'S VARIOUS, UH, PROBLEMS.

Panel 3: BUT AS SOON AS HE TOOK THE OATH OF OFFICE, THE *REAL* BARACK OBAMA EMERGED.

--AND BY EXECUTIVE PRESIDENTIAL ORDER, I AM DECLARING THE UNITED STATES A *SOCIALIST MUSLIM DICTATORSHIP!*

HE CAN DO THAT?

OF COURSE! HAVE YOU EVER *READ* THE CONSTITUTION?

Panel 4: BILL AYERS WAS SOON APPOINTED AS CHIEF GOVERNMENT BOMBER IN CHARGE OF BOMBING GOVERNMENT BUILDINGS!

YOU THERE! I WANT THE WASHINGTON MEMORIAL BLOWN UP-- *PRONTO!*

RIGHT AWAY, SIR!

Panel 5: AMERICANS WERE REQUIRED TO MEMORIZE THE RECORDED SERMONS OF JEREMIAH WRIGHT-- AND PUNISHED WITH *HIGHER TAXES* IF THEY *FAILED!*

AND...UH...AMERICA'S CHICKENS HAVE COME HOME...TO *LIVE?*

SORRY! YOUR TAX RATE JUST WENT UP BY *FOUR PERCENT!*

Panel 6: AND AS IT TURNED OUT, THAT INFAMOUS NEW YORKER COVER WAS NOTHING IF NOT *PRESCIENT.*

WE'RE LUCKY IT DIDN'T COST US THE *ELECTION!*

INDEED WE ARE! NOW TOSS ANOTHER AMERICAN FLAG ON THE FIRE AND LET'S FIGURE OUT WHERE TO HANG OUR CHERISHED PORTRAIT OF *OSAMA BIN LADEN!*

TOM TOMORROW©2008... www.thismodernworld.com

THIS MODERN WORLD

by TOM TOMORROW

ATTACK OF THE INVISIBLE HAND OF THE FREE MARKET

IF IT'S INVISIBLE, WHY CAN WE **SEE** IT?

NEVER MIND THAT--JUST **RUN!!**

IT BEGINS IN A SECRET LAB... WHERE AN ELITE TEAM OF ECONOMISTS KEEP WATCH OVER THE MYSTERIOUS **HAND...**

IT'S GROWING **RAPIDLY!** I WONDER IF WE SHOULD REGULATE ITS CONSUMPTION OF **MORTGAGE-BACKED SECURITIES!**

WHAT AN ABSURD SUGGESTION! ARE YOU **SURE** YOU'RE AN ELITE ECONOMIST?

system status: normal

DOWN THE ROAD, A DISTRAUGHT STRANGER RUSHES TO WARN LOCAL AUTHORITIES OF AN IMPENDING **CATASTROPHE...**

GASP--HOUSING BUBBLE--PANT PANT--DERIVATIVES--PANT PANT-- THINGS MAN WAS NOT MEANT TO **MEDDLE** WITH--WHEEZE GASP--

UH OH! SOUNDS LIKE SOMEBODY HAD ONE TOO **MANY!**

HE CAN SLEEP IT OFF IN THE **TANK!**

WANTED

AND THEN--SUDDENLY--

SOMETHING IS **HAPPENING!** THE INVISIBLE HAND OF THE FREE MARKET IS HAVING AN **ADVERSE REACTION** TO ITS STEADY DIET OF **SUBPRIME LOANS!**

NO ONE COULD HAVE FORESEEN **THIS!** ONLY **SEVEN HUNDRED BILLION DOLLARS** CAN SAVE US **NOW!**

BUT THE DESPERATE INFUSION OF TAXPAYER FUNDS ISN'T **ENOUGH!**

THE HAND HAS BROKEN **FREE!** IT'S ON A **RAMPAGE**--DESTROYING EVERY HOME AND BUSINESS IN ITS **PATH!**

THIS IS NOT RATIONAL BEHAVIOR AT **ALL!**

AND AS THE HAND WREAKS HAVOC, CITIZENS HAVE ONLY ONE PLACE TO TURN FOR HELP.

YOUR **ONLY HOPE** IS TO KEEP THROWING HUNDREDS OF BILLIONS OF DOLLARS AT THE PROBLEM--**INDEFINITELY!**

TRUST US! WE'RE **ECONOMISTS!**

AND REMEMBER-- **NO ONE** COULD HAVE SEEN THIS COMING!

STAY TUNED FOR THE **THRILLING CONCLUSION** (AS IF YOU HAVE A CHOICE!)

TOM TOMORROW©2008... www.thismodernworld.com

THIS MODERN WORLD

by TOM TOMORROW

THE BUSH YEARS: A LOOK BACK

AFTER THE TERROR ATTACKS OF 9-11, THE PRESIDENT *RUSHED* BACK TO THE WHITE HOUSE TO GIVE AN IMPROMPTU, UNSCRIPTED SPEECH TO THE NATION.

THOSE WHO FUNDED AND COORDINATED THIS ACT OF VILE DEPRAVITY WILL BE APPREHENDED AND TRIED IN A A *COURT OF LAW*--IN KEEPING WITH OUR FUNDAMENTAL PRINCIPLES AS A NATION!

HE MADE IT CLEAR THAT THIS WAS NO TIME FOR PARTISANSHIP.

HIGH-RANKING MEMBERS OF MY ADMINISTRATION *HAVE* ADVISED ME TO USE THIS TRAGEDY AS AN EXCUSE TO EMBARK ON A RECKLESS MISSION OF IMPERIAL HUBRIS.

I HAVE ASKED FOR THEIR IMMEDIATE RESIGNATIONS.

HIS MEASURED RESPONSE SET A TONE OF RATIONALITY FOR THE COMING YEARS.

WE'VE GOT TO GO BOMB *SOMEBODY*--JUST TO SHOW WE *CAN!*

WHAT'S UP WITH *THAT* GUY?

IT'S A GOOD THING NO ONE LISTENS TO *HIM!*

IT WAS AN UNCERTAIN TIME, TO BE SURE...BUT AMERICANS NEVER FORGOT THEIR CORE VALUES.

CHECK *THIS* OUT! THIS NUTCASE BLOGGER THINKS WE SHOULD SIMPLY *DISREGARD* HUMAN RIGHTS AND CIVIL LIBERTIES!

IF HE THINKS STALINIST RUSSIA WAS SO GREAT, HE SHOULD INVENT A TIME MACHINE AND GO *LIVE* THERE!

AND THE ADMINISTRATION NEVER WAVERED IN ITS COMMITMENT TO DIPLOMACY AND INTERNATIONAL COOPERATION.

--AND I WANT TO THANK OUR ALLIES FOR THEIR HELP IN DISCREDITING RUMORS OF WMD'S IN IRAQ, A COUNTRY WHICH POSES NO MORE THREAT TO US THAN THIS HARMLESS VIAL OF *SALT!*

SO IT'S REALLY NO WONDER THAT THE REPUBLICAN PARTY WAS SO OVERWHELMINGLY VICTORIOUS IN THE ELECTIONS OF 2008.

THEY'VE DONE SUCH AN AMAZING JOB SO *FAR*--WHY WOULD WE WANT ANYONE *ELSE* RUNNING THINGS?

AND WITH THE RISE OF VICE-PRESIDENT *PALIN*--WISE LEADERSHIP IS GUARANTEED FOR *YEARS TO COME!*

TOM TOMORROW©2008... www.thismodernworld.com

THIS MODERN WORLD

by TOM TOMORROW

2008 YEAR IN REVIEW

A WHOLLY SUBJECTIVE AND THOROUGHLY INCOMPLETE LOOK BACK AT THE YEAR THAT WAS

PART ONE: GOODBYE TO ALL THAT

JAN. 4: JOHN MCCAIN SUGGESTS MASSIVELY UNPOPULAR IRAQ WAR COULD BE PROLONGED BY "100 YEARS."

HEH HEH! DO I KNOW HOW TO WIN AN ELECTION OR *WHAT?*

JAN. 7: BILL "WRONG ABOUT EVERYTHING" KRISTOL BEGINS NEW COLUMN IN N.Y. TIMES WITH A MISATTRIBUTED QUOTE.

I HOPE THIS DOES NOT IMPACT MY HARD-WON *CREDIBILITY!*

JAN. 10: BUSH AIDES PREDICT THE PRESIDENT WILL LEAVE OFFICE WITH A 45% APPROVAL RATING.

ALSO THERE WILL BE UNICORNS. AND MAGIC RAINBOWS.

JAN. 11: WASH. POST REPORTS TELECOMS REPEATEDLY CUT OFF WIRETAPS DUE TO FBI'S FAILURE TO PAY BILLS ON TIME.

IGNORE THE CONSTITUTION ALL YOU *WANT*--

--BUT DON'T IGNORE OUR "LATE PAYMENT" NOTICES!

JAN. 18: SEAN HANNITY DECLARES "THE ECONOMY IS *PHENOMENAL!*"

IF YOU DON'T BELIEVE *ME*, JUST ASK MY *ACCOUNTANT!*

FEB. 4: KARL ROVE JOINS FOX NEWS.

SERIOUSLY, WHAT CAN WE ADD TO THAT?

FEB. 28: EASILY-ALARMED FALAFEL ENTHUSIAST BILL O'REILLY WARNS OF--

"--THE SIMILARITIES BETWEEN WHAT HITLER...DID BACK THEN AND THE HATE-FILLED BLOGS, WHAT THEY'RE DOING *NOW!*"

FEB. 28: GEORGE BUSH IS SURPRISED TO LEARN THAT GAS MAY SOON HIT $4 A GALLON.

"THAT'S *INTERESTIN'!* I HADN'T *HEARD* THAT!"

FEB. 28, SAME PRESS CONFERENCE: BUSH DODGES QUESTION ABOUT DONATIONS TO HIS LIBRARY, STATING--

"I...HAVE BEEN FOCUSED ELSEWHERE--LIKE ON *GASOLINE PRICES!*"

MARCH 1: BILL "WRONG ABOUT EVERYTHING" KRISTOL PREDICTS--

"IT'S GOING TO BE A *NATIONAL SECURITY* ELECTION!"

MARCH 18: JOHN MCCAIN--A MAN RUNNING FOR *PRESIDENT*--REPEATEDLY CONFUSES SUNNIS AND SHIITES.

ALL I KNOW IS, THEY *BOTH* BETTER STAY OFF *MY* LAWNS!

APRIL 14: ASKED IF OBAMA IS A MARXIST, JOE LIEBERMAN REPLIES--

"I MUST SAY, THAT'S A *GOOD QUESTION!*"

APRIL 24: RUSH LIMBAUGH FANTASIZES ABOUT VIOLENCE AT THE D.N.C.

"I AM DREAMING OF *RIOTS!*"

HIS DREAMS ARE NOT DESTINED TO BE REALIZED.

MAY 8: HILLARY CLINTON EXPLAINS THAT SHE IS MORE POPULAR THAN OBAMA AMONG "WORKING, HARDWORKING AMERICANS, WHITE AMERICANS."

HEH HEH-- DID I SAY THAT OUT *LOUD?*

JUNE 29: BILL "WRONG ABOUT EVERYTHING" KRISTOL ENTHUSIASTICALLY PROMOTES *SARAH PALIN* FOR REPUBLICAN V.P.

TRUST ME-- SHE'S THE *PERFECT CHOICE!*

...TO BE CONTINUED!

TOM TOMORROW ©2008

THIS MODERN WORLD

by TOM TOMORROW

2008 YEAR IN REVIEW

A WHOLLY SUBJECTIVE AND THOROUGHLY INCOMPLETE LOOK BACK AT THE YEAR THAT WAS

PART TWO: THE END OF AN ERROR

JULY 7: JOHN McCAIN REVEALS HIS PLAN TO BALANCE THE BUDGET.

WE'LL USE THE MONEY WE SAVE BY WINNING THE WARS IN IRAQ AND AFGHANISTAN!

SERIOUSLY, THAT'S MY PLAN.

JULY 30: OBAMA SUGGESTS KEEPING YOUR TIRES PROPERLY INFLATED; CONSERVATIVES FIND THIS *HILARIOUS.*

WHAT **NEXT**? REGULAR *OIL CHANGES*?

AUG. 21: McCAIN IS ASKED HOW MANY HOUSES HE OWNS.

"I THINK-- I'LL HAVE MY STAFF GET BACK TO YOU!"

CONSERVATIVES DENOUNCE THE "GOTCHA" MEDIA.

EARLY SEPT.: THE R.N.C. SPENDS OVER $150,000 ON PALIN FAMILY WARDROBE, INCLUDING SILK BOXERS FOR TODD.

I ONLY WEAR THEM FOR THE GOOD OF THE CAMPAIGN!

SEPT. 2: JOE LIEBERMAN ENDORSES THE McCAIN/PALIN TICKET IN A PRIME TIME SPEECH AT THE REPUBLICAN CONVENTION.

SUCK ON *THIS*, NED LAMONT!

SEPT. 10: OBAMA USES THE EXPRESSION "LIPSTICK ON A PIG"; CONSERVATIVES SPEND A WEEK PRETENDING TO BE OUTRAGED.

CAN YOU **BELIEVE** HE CALLED SARAH PALIN A **PIG** THESE LIBERALS I GOTTA TELL YA IT'S JUST *SHOCKING*

SEPT. 15, MORNING: McCAIN SAYS FUNDAMENTALS OF ECONOMY ARE *STRONG!*

SEPT. 15, AFTERNOON: McCAIN SAYS FUNDAMENTALS ARE AT *GREAT RISK!*

SEPT. 17: LADY LYNN FORESTER DE ROTHSCHILD CALLS OBAMA AN "ELITIST," ENDORSES McCAIN.

SEPT. 18: LADY DE ROTHSCHILD EXPLAINS ON CNN THAT OBAMA DOES NOT RESPECT "THE PEOPLE... WHO ARE THE REDNECKS OR WHOEVER."

SEPT. 30: SARAH PALIN IS ASKED WHAT NEWSPAPERS AND MAGAZINES SHE READS.

"UM--ALL OF THEM!"

AGAIN, THE "GOTCHA" MEDIA ARE TO BLAME.

OCT. 1: LATEST TOM TOMORROW COMPILATION IS RELEASED, BECOMES IMMEDIATE BESTSELLER.

THE FUTURE'S SO BRIGHT I CAN'T BEAR TO LOOK

WHAT? YOU DIDN'T HEAR ABOUT THAT?

OCT. 12: BARACK OBAMA THREATENS TO LOWER A PLUMBER'S TAXES, MUCH TO PLUMBER'S APPARENT DISMAY.

YOU'LL NEVER GET AWAY WITH THIS, YOU--YOU *SOCIALIST!*

NOV. 4: AMERICANS VOTE TO END LONG NATIONAL NIGHTMARE; PUNDITS BEGIN 2012 SPECULATION.

WILL SARAH PALIN CHOOSE JOE THE PLUMBER AS HER *RUNNING MATE*?

NOV. 18: DEMOCRATS VERY STERNLY ALLOW JOE LIEBERMAN TO KEEP HIS CHAIRMANSHIP.

I'VE CERTAINLY LEARNED *MY* LESSON!

NOV. 25: N.Y. POST REPORTS THAT DUE TO A BROKEN JAW, ANN COULTER'S MOUTH HAS BEEN WIRED SHUT.

MMRPH! MRRPH *MMRPH!*

ATHEISTS EVERYWHERE ARE GIVEN MOMENTARY PAUSE.

DECEMBER: COLLAPSE OF CAPITALISM CONTINUES; BLAGOJEVICH SCANDAL ERUPTS; CHRISTMAS WARRIOR BILL O'REILLY CONTINUES HIS LONELY STRUGGLE.

HO HO HO, DAMMIT.

...SEE YOU NEXT YEAR!

TOM TOMORROW©2008

THIS MODERN WORLD

by TOM TOMORROW

HEY, WHAT'S GOIN' *ON*? I'VE BEEN *CARTOONIFIED!*

YEP! IN HONOR OF YOUR IMMINENT DEPARTURE FROM THE OVAL OFFICE, YOU'VE BEEN RESTORED TO OUR INITIAL FEBRUARY 2000 CARICATURE OF YOU AS *ALFRED E. NEUMAN!**

*SUBSEQUENTLY "CO-OPTED" BY *THE NATION.*

LITTLE DID WE KNOW WHAT WAS IN STORE FOR US, BACK THEN... I MEAN, THIS CARTOON USED TO TAKE A WEEK AWAY FROM POLITICS EVERY NOW AND AGAIN, FOR CULTURAL COMMENTARY, OR JUST TO BE GOOFY FOR THE HELL OF IT--BUT NOT SINCE *YOU* TOOK OFFICE!

I SWEAR, I HAVEN'T HAD A CHANCE TO CATCH MY BREATH IN *EIGHT YEARS!*

THINK ABOUT IT--

--BUSH V. GORE, CHENEY'S ENERGY TASK FORCE, KENNY BOY LAY, PUTIN'S SOUL, "BIN LADEN DETERMINED TO STRIKE," 9-11, AXIS OF EVIL, FREEDOM FRIES, PATRIOT ACT, INDEFINITE DETENTION, EXTRAORDINARY RENDITION, GUANTANAMO, YELLOWCAKE URANIUM, SHOCK AND AWE, MISSION ACCOMPLISHED, HALLIBURTON, BLACKWATER, JESSICA LYNCH, PAT TILLMAN, BAGRAM, ABU GHRAIB, WATERBOARDING, SWIFTBOATING, TAX CUTS, SOARING DEFICITS, TERRY SCHIAVO, STEM CELL RESEARCH, DOMESTIC SURVEILLANCE, TELECOM IMMUNITY, HURRICANE KATRINA, THE COLLAPSE OF CAPITALISM AS WE KNOW IT, AND KARL ROVE. *KARL ROVE!*

AND THAT'S JUST OFF THE TOP OF MY HEAD.

WELL, AT LEAST I GAVE YA LOTS OF *MATERIAL!* HEH HEH HEH!

TRUE ENOUGH! AND SPEAKING AS BOTH A POLITICAL HUMORIST AND A CITIZEN OF THIS COUNTRY, LET ME SAY WITH ALL THE SINCERITY I CAN MUSTER--

--*DON'T LET THE DOOR HIT YOU IN THE ASS ON YOUR WAY OUT!!*

SLAM!!

BOY, WAS *THAT* SATISFYING!

HAPPY NEW YEAR, EVERYONE!

Tom Tomorrow©2008

THIS MODERN WORLD

by TOM TOMORROW

A FAREWELL SALUTE...

©TOM TOMORROW... FOR THE LONG-AWAITED WEEK OF 1-20-09

THIS MODERN WORLD

by TOM TOMORROW

Panel 1:
IN SOME ALTERNATE UNIVERSE, AMERICANS ARE ABOUT TO BEGIN A PAINFUL PERIOD OF INTENSIVE NATIONAL SOUL-SEARCHING.

WE SAW THE PHOTOS FROM ABU GHRAIB--WE HEARD ABOUT WATER-BOARDING AND WORSE--AND ALL WE DID WAS ARGUE ABOUT THE *SEMANTICS* OF TORTURE?

WHAT KIND OF MONSTERS *WERE* WE?

Panel 2:
THEIR NEW PRESIDENT WILL INITIATE A THOROUGH INVESTIGATION OF THE PREVIOUS ADMINISTRATION'S MISDEEDS.

WE'LL ALL JOIN TOGETHER IN, UH, POST-PARTISAN *UNITY*--

--JUST AS SOON AS WE FIGURE OUT EXACTLY WHAT THESE SCUM-BAG CRIMINALS HAVE BEEN *DOING* FOR THE PAST EIGHT YEARS!

Panel 3:
AFTER EIGHT LONG YEARS, THE WALLS OF SECRECY WILL BEGIN TO CRUMBLE.

SO DICK CHENEY USED THAT "MAN-SIZED SAFE" IN HIS OFFICE TO STORE *LIVE VICTIMS* FOR HIS UNSPEAKABLE RITUALS OF HUMAN *SACRIFICE*?

BOY ARE THE LATE-NIGHT COMEDIANS GOING TO HAVE A FIELD DAY WITH *THAT*!

Panel 4:
THE NATION'S LEGAL SYSTEM WILL RISE TO THE CHALLENGE, PROVING THAT NO ONE IS ABOVE THE LAW.

--IN AN IRONIC TWIST, THE DIS-GRACED FORMER PRESIDENT AND VICE-PRESIDENT WILL SERVE OUT THEIR TERMS AT THE NOW-VACANT *GUANTANAMO* FACILITY!

KARL ROVE, MEANWHILE, REMAINS A FUGITIVE, AND SHOULD BE CONSIDERED *ARMED* AND EXTREMELY *MACHIAVELLIAN*!

Action McNews Network

Panel 5:
AND YET, A COLLECTIVE SENSE OF NATIONAL SHAME WILL LINGER FOR A GENERATION OR MORE.

YOU--YOU'RE A *GEORGE BUSH*!

YEAH, WELL--*YOU'RE* A *DICK CHENEY*!

CHILDREN! WATCH YOUR LANGUAGE!

Panel 6:
OF COURSE, NONE OF THIS WILL HAPPEN IN *OUR* UNIVERSE.

MISTAKES WERE MADE--BUT WHAT'S DONE IS DONE! NO POINT IN WORRY-ING ABOUT IT *NOW*!

YOU'D HAVE TO BE A FAR-LEFT *WACKO* TO THINK OTHER-WISE!

AND IF YOU *WERE*, NO ONE WOULD *CARE* WHAT YOU THINK!

TOM TOMORROW©2009

32

by TOM TOMORROW

THIS MODERN WORLD

by TOM TOMORROW

AH, MOONBAT! WELCOME TO THE NEW **BASEMENT HEADQUARTERS** OF MY BOY DETECTIVE AGENCY! IT'S **MUCH** BETTER FORTIFIED THAN THE OLD TREEHOUSE, IN THE EVENT OF WIDESPREAD SOCIAL DISORDER AMONG THE LOWER CLASSES!

UM--ARE YOU OKAY? YOUR MOM SAYS YOU'VE BEEN SPENDING A LOT OF TIME DOWN HERE...

INDEED I **HAVE**, MOONBAT! I'M HOT ON THE TRAIL OF ONE OF HISTORY'S **GREATEST COVERUPS!**

YOU SEE, I RECENTLY BEGAN TO WONDER WHY LIBERALS WERE **STILL** TALKING ABOUT GEORGE W. BUSH--EVEN THOUGH HE IS **NO LONGER** IN **OFFICE!**

UH--BECAUSE HE'S ONLY BEEN GONE A MONTH, AND HE LEFT THE COUNTRY IN HORRIBLE SHAPE--?

OH, MOONBAT! SOMEDAY I REALLY MUST INTRODUCE YOU TO MY CLOSE PERSONAL FRIEND, **REALITY!** NO, AS MY INTERNET INVESTIGATIONS SOON REVEALED, IT IS BECAUSE THEY WANT TO DRAW ATTENTION AWAY FROM THE **REAL** CULPRIT OF THE ECONOMIC CRISIS--

--**JIMMY CARTER!** THE SINISTER PLAN **HE** SET INTO MOTION MORE THAN THIRTY YEARS AGO HAS FINALLY REACHED ITS CULMINATION-- AND HAPLESS REPUBLICANS HAVE BEEN **POWERLESS** TO STOP IT!

ER--SO **BUSH** IS IRRELEVANT-- BUT **JIMMY CARTER**--

SILENCE, MOONBAT! THAT'S ONLY THE **BEGINNING!**

FROM THERE, I UNCOVERED A MASSIVE CONSPIRACY STRETCHING BACK **DECADES**--ENCOMPASSING SEVERAL GENERATIONS OF LIBERAL ACADEMICS AND JOURNALISTS-- ALL WORKING IN TANDEM TO CONCEAL FROM THE AMERICAN PUBLIC THE STUNNING HISTORICAL TRUTH--

--THAT F.D.R. **CAUSED** THE GREAT DEPRESSION--WITH HIS **LIBERAL SPENDING PROGRAMS!!**

YOU KNOW, YOU REALLY MIGHT WANT TO THINK ABOUT LEAVING THE BASEMENT OCCASIONALLY.

HAH! DO YOU THINK ALL THIS DETECTIVE WORK IS GOING TO DO **ITSELF?**

NEXT: GROVER CLEVELAND'S RESPONSIBILITY FOR THE **TARP** FIASCO!

THIS MODERN WORLD

by TOM TOMORROW

THE IRAQ WAR, GLOBAL CLIMATE CHANGE, FREE MARKET TRIUMPHALISM--SUDDENLY CONSERVATIVES ARE WIDELY ACKNOWLEDGED TO HAVE BEEN ENTIRELY WRONG ABOUT *EVERYTHING*.

YES, WELL, MISTAKES WERE MADE-- BUT NONE OF THAT MATTERS *NOW*!

HOW DO YOU FIGURE?

HAVEN'T YOU *HEARD*? WE'VE ENTERED A NEW ERA OF *POST-PARTISAN* POLITICS, SYMBOLIZED BY OBAMA'S CHOICE OF AN ANTI-GAY FUNDAMENTALIST TO DELIVER THE INAUGURAL INVOCATION--MUCH TO THE DISMAY OF THE INTOLERANT *LEFT*!

YES, WE'RE SHOCKINGLY IN-TOLERANT OF INTOLERANCE.

EVERYONE AGREES--IT'S TIME TO PUT THE DIVISIVENESS OF THE PAST *BEHIND* US! IT DOESN'T MATTER *WHO'S* RESPONSIBLE FOR FOR THE PROBLEMS WE FACE! WE CAN'T BE OBSESSED WITH CASTING *BLAME*! IT'S TIME TO LOOK TO THE *FUTURE*--NOT THE *PAST*!

FUNNY HOW THIS ONLY SEEMS TO HAPPEN WHEN *REPUBLICANS* LOSE AN ELECTION.

TUT TUT! THAT DOESN'T SOUND VERY POST-PARTISAN TO *ME*!

Tom Tomorrow©2009

THIS MODERN WORLD

by TOM TOMORROW

there's that melody again

WITH A DEMOCRAT IN OFFICE, THE ESTABLISHMENT MEDIA STRIKE UP A REFRAIN WE HAVEN'T HEARD IN, OH, EIGHT YEARS OR SO...

--AND WILL PRESIDENT OBAMA RISE ABOVE *IDEOLOGY* AND IN-CLUDE THE REPUBLICANS AS *EQUAL PARTNERS* IN EVERY DECISION HE *MAKES*?

IT'S REALLY THE ONLY *RESPONSIBLE* THING TO DO!

HOW DEEPLY THIS MESSAGE RES-ONATES WITH OBAMA HAS LONG BEEN A SUBJECT OF DEBATE AMONG HIS SUPPORTERS.

HE *SAYS* HE WANTS TO WORK WITH REPUBLICANS--BUT IN OUR *IMAG-INARY* CONVERSATIONS HE ASSURES ME HE DOES NOT *MEAN* IT!

MAYBE HE DOESN'T NOT WANT TO *NOT* WORK WITH THEM!

BUT WHAT IF THAT'S WHAT HE *WANTS* US TO NOT THINK?

BUT CLEARLY--EVEN AFTER A BLOWOUT ELECTION--DEMOCRATS FEEL THEY MUST EMPHASIZE *HARMONY*...

IT IS TIME TO EXTEND A BIPAR-TISAN HAND ACROSS THE AISLE--AND WORK WITH OUR REPUBLI-CAN FRIENDS TO FIND *COMMON GROUND*!

PARTISANSHIP IS *SO* DISTASTEFUL!

...WHILE REPUBLICANS REMAIN AS NOISY AND DISSONANT AS EVER.

WE'LL VOTE AGAINST *ANY PRO-POSAL* THE DEMOCRATS COME UP WITH UNLESS *SIGNIFICANT* CON-CESSIONS ARE MADE TO APPEASE US!

AND THEN WE'LL *STILL* VOTE AGAINST IT!

MAINLY, WE JUST HOPE THIS DOESN'T END UP TURNING INTO THE SAME OLD SONG AND DANCE.

HEY GUYS! HERE'S MY TIMID, IN-CREMENTAL *HEALTH CARE PRO-POSAL*, WHICH I'VE TWISTED INTO *KNOTS* TO AVOID UNWARRANTED ACCUSATIONS OF "SOCIALISM"!

TOO BAD-- *SOCIALIST*!

JOINK!

TOM TOMORROW©2009

THIS MODERN WORLD

by TOM TOMORROW

G.O.P. STRATEGIES FOR SUCCESS

1. BLAME THE VICTIMS. ANYONE SUFFERING IN THIS ECONOMY IS A *LOSER!*

THE WEAK MUST ALWAYS BE CULLED FROM THE HERD!

2. HIGHLIGHT REPUBLICAN FAILURES AS VALIDATION OF ANTI-GOVERNMENT IDEOLOGY. *OUR* STAGGERINGLY INCOMPETENT RESPONSE TO KATRINA--

--PROVES THAT *WASHINGTON* CAN'T DO *ANYTHING* RIGHT!

3. DEVELOP INSULAR MYTHOLOGY INCOMPREHENSIBLE TO LAYPEOPLE. FANNIE MAE! BARNEY FRANK! HIGH SPEED RAIL! ACORN! *ACORN!!*

UH--OKAY...

4. STAND UP FOR THE BIG GUYS. HOW *DARE* OBAMA TELL CEO'S HOW TO SPEND THEIR BAILOUT MONEY!

WHAT'S THIS COUNTRY *COMING* TO?

5. REPETITION--YOUR KEY TO *VICTORY!* SOCIALISM SOCIALISM *SOCIALISM* SOCIALISM!

SOCIALISM SOCIALISM SOCIALISM!

6. EMBRACE IGNORANCE. WE DON'T NEED NO CANDIDATES WITH NO FANCY *BOOK LEARNIN'!*

ME NOT EVEN KNOW WHAT BOOKS *AM!*

7. PUT FORTH ABRASIVE, THRICE-DIVORCED FORMER DRUG ADDICT AS PUBLIC FACE OF PARTY. WE'RE ALL ABOUT THE *FAMILY VALUES!*

8. PRETEND THE LAST EIGHT YEARS NEVER HAPPENED. I DO NOT KNOW THIS PRESIDENT "BUSH" OF WHOM YOU SPEAK.

PERHAPS YOU MEAN "CLINTON"-- OR "CARTER"?

9. INSIST THAT FAILED POLICIES WILL WORK IF TRIED AGAIN. TAX CUTS FOR THE WEALTHY HAVE NEVER BEEN *PROPERLY IMPLEMENTED!*

HENCE OUR CURRENT TURMOIL!

10. REMEMBER: NOTHING WINS VOTERS OVER LIKE *HYSTERICAL PARANOIA!* IT'S ALL A *PLOT!* OBAMA WANTS TO *DESTROY* AMERICA!

HE DOESN'T EVEN HAVE A *BIRTH CERTIFICATE!*

11. JUST SAY NO. THE PRESIDENT WANTS--

FORGET IT! IT'S A TERRIBLE IDEA! I VEHEMENTLY OPPOSE IT!

WHATEVER IT IS!

TOM TOMORROW©2009

THIS MODERN WORLD

by TOM TOMORROW

THE FUTURE

WHERE YOU AND I WILL SPEND THE REST OF OUR LIVES

AS THE NEW MILLENIUM PROGRESSES, THE INCREASINGLY BELEAGURED NEWS INDUSTRY BEGINS TO EMULATE THE *HUFFINGTON POST'S* PIONEERING BUSINESS MODEL.

THIS IS *GREAT!* WHY PAY RE-PORTERS--WHEN WE CAN JUST LINK TO *OTHER* PEOPLE'S REPORT-ING FOR *FREE*?

I DON'T SEE *ANYTHING* THAT COULD GO WRONG WITH *THIS* STRATEGY!

AFTER THE LAST REPORTER FILES THE LAST NEWS STORY, AN ARMY OF *CITIZEN* JOURNALISTS GAMELY TRY TO FILL THE VOID.

MY STUNNING EXPOSÉ OF NOISY GARBAGEMEN WHO WAKE ME UP AT SIX A.M. IS GONNA RIP THE *LID* OFF THE SANITATION DEPARTMENT!

WAIT TILL YOU SEE *MY* INVESTIGATIVE REPORT ON RANDOM SERVICE EMPLOYEES WHO ANNOY ME!

HAH! WHO NEEDS THE M.S.M. *ANY-WAY*?

BUT EVENTUALLY, BLOGGERS ARE LEFT WITH ONLY *ONE REMAINING FACT* ABOUT WHICH TO OPINE.

HAVE YOU READ CHICKENPOTPIE'S CRITIQUE OF HIS SUPREME MAJESTY FRED THE FIRST'S TAKEDOWN OF FARTYBUTT'S POST ABOUT THE SOAR-ING RAVIOLI BEAST'S ATTEMPT TO *RECONTEXTUALIZE* THE ONE REMAINING FACT?

READ IT? I'VE ALREADY *REFUTED* IT ON *MY* BLOG!

BUT THEN THE BLOGS ARE SUP-PLANTED BY *TWEETS*--WHICH ARE NOW LIMITED TO A *SINGLE WORD*, JUST TO KEEP THINGS *EXTRA* SIMPLE.

HAPPY

SAD

BORED

AND OF COURSE, *CARTOONS* HAVE LONG SINCE BEEN RENDERED OBSOLETE BY THOSE ENDLESSLY AMUSING *LOLCATS*.

HA, HA! THIS TYPO-PRONE CAT WANTS A CHEESEBURGER--WITH *PICKLES*!

IT DOESN'T GET ANY FUNNIER THAN *THAT*!

AT LEAST, NOT ANY-MORE.

TOM TOMORROW©2009

THIS MODERN WORLD

by TOM TOMORROW

DYSTOPIAN POST-APOCALYPTIC MOVIES

vs

DYSTOPIAN POST-APOCALYPTIC REALITY

MOVIES: HUBRISTIC SCIENTISTS AND/OR POLITICIANS UNLEASH DEVASTATION ON UNSUSPECTING WORLD.

WHAT COULD POSSIBLY GO WRONG IN OUR *DEADLY BIOWEAPONS RESEARCH FACILITY?*

REALITY: HUBRISTIC INVESTMENT BANKERS UNLEASH DEVASTATION ON UNSUSPECTING WORLD.

WHAT COULD POSSIBLY GO WRONG WITH OUR *COLLATERALIZED DEBT OBLIGATIONS?*

MOVIES: MUCH OF HUMANITY IS WIPED OUT.

YOU *MANIACS!* YOU BLEW IT *UP!*

REALITY: MUCH OF HUMANITY'S ASSETS ARE WIPED OUT.

YOU BLEW UP MY *401-K!*

GOSH DARN YOU TO *HECK!*

MOVIES: A LONE SURVIVOR EKES OUT A MARGINAL EXISTENCE IN THE RUINS OF AN EMPTY CITY.

I CAN HOLD ON UNTIL MY SUPPLIES RUN OUT--BUT WHAT *THEN?*

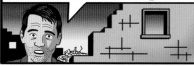

REALITY: MILLIONS OF LOAN SURVIVORS EKE OUT A MARGINAL EXISTENCE IN THE RUINS OF EMPTY SUBURBS.

I CAN HOLD ON UNTIL MY SAVINGS RUN OUT--BUT WHAT *THEN?*

MOVIES: MUTANT ZOMBIES DOMINATE A NIGHTMARE LANDSCAPE!

OH MY GOD, THEY'RE *EVERYWHERE!* THERE'S NOWHERE *SAFE!*

REALITY: ZOMBIE BANKS DOMINATE A NIGHTMARE LANDSCAPE!

OH MY GOD, THEY'RE *EVERYWHERE!* THERE'S NOWHERE SAFE TO PUT MY *MONEY!*

Bank of America   citibank

MOVIES: THE FUTURE HANGS BY A THREAD.

THIS FRAGILE GLASS VIAL OF SERUM... IS HUMANITY'S *ONLY HOPE!*

REALITY: SAME DEAL.

PRESIDENT OBAMA'S CAUTIOUS STIMULUS PLAN...IS THE ECONOMY'S *ONLY HOPE!*

NEXT: SOYLENT GREEN IS...*PEOPLE'S RETIREMENT ACCOUNTS!!*

TOM TOMORROW©2009

THIS MODERN WORLD

by TOM TOMORROW

The Genius of Capitalism

with your host -- the Invisible Hand!

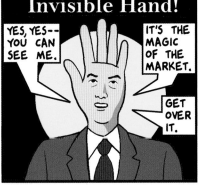

YES, YES-- YOU CAN SEE ME.

IT'S THE MAGIC OF THE MARKET.

GET OVER IT.

STEP ONE: INDUSTRIOUS WALL ST. TRADERS INVENT FANTASTIC NEW WAYS TO CREATE WEALTH!

WE'VE CREATED FINANCIAL INSTRUMENTS TOO COMPLEX FOR THE HUMAN MIND TO **COMPREHEND!**

WE HAVE **NO IDEA** WHAT WE'RE DOING--BUT WE'RE MAKING A **BUNDLE!**

WOW! THAT'S WHAT **I** CALL INNOVATION!

RIOTIC ESTMEN'S UP

STEP TWO: WHEN THINGS DON'T WORK OUT **QUITE** AS WELL AS PLANNED, THE GOVERNMENT STEPS IN!

PLEASE ACCEPT THIS INITIAL BAILOUT OF SEVERAL HUNDRED BILLION DOLLARS--WITH OUR **COMPLIMENTS!**

WELL, OKAY--BUT ONLY IF YOU PROMISE NOT TO USE THE "N" WORD!*

ANYTHING YOU SAY, SIR!

LOADING DOCK

*NATIONALIZATION, OF COURSE!

STEP THREE: FLUSH WITH CASH, TRADERS QUITE REASONABLY AWARD THEMSELVES BONUSES. INEXPLICABLE PUBLIC OUTCRY ENSUES.

DON'T THEY **UNDERSTAND?** WE'RE THE ONLY ONES WHO CAN **CLEAN UP** THE MESS WE MADE!

GOOD POINT! AND BESIDES-- IT'S NOT LIKE YOU DESTROYED THE **ENTIRE** WORLD ECONOMY!

PATRI IC INVEST ENTS GROUP

STEP FOUR: FIRMS ARE EVENTUALLY FORCED TO REPAY BONUSES (IN PART OR FULL) AS A MATTER OF POLITICAL EXPEDIENCY.

OH, FOR CHRISSAKES, YOU WANT YOUR $165 MILLION BACK? FINE. SOMEBODY GET ME THE KEY TO THE PETTY CASH DRAWER.

I'M GLAD YOU'VE SEEN THE ERROR OF YOUR WAYS!

RIGHT, SURE, WHATEVER.

STEP FIVE: CONTROVERSY DIES DOWN, FREEING THE ADMINISTRATION TO FUNNEL HUNDREDS OF BILLIONS **MORE** TO STRUGGLING BANKERS!

HERE'S ANOTHER GIGANTIC TRUCKLOAD OF MONEY! DON'T SPEND IT ALL IN ONE PLACE! HA HA!

HA HA!

I JUST LOVE A HAPPY ENDING--DON'T **YOU?**

LOADING DOCK

TOM TOMORROW©2009

THIS MODERN WORLD

by TOM TOMORROW

Panel 1:

THE PROBLEM: BANKS ARE LOADED DOWN WITH BAD INVESTMENTS THEY ARE UNABLE TO SELL FOR THE ARTIFICALLY INFLATED PRICES THEY WOULD PREFER TO RECEIVE!

IT'S A DRAIN ON OUR ENTIRE ECONOMY! AND OBVIOUSLY THE GOVERNMENT CANNOT INTERVENE *DIRECTLY*, LEST WE INVOKE THE SPECTRE OF *NATIONALIZATION*!

TRULY, NOTHING COULD BE MORE TERRIFYING!

Panel 2:

THE SOLUTION: LOAN A HALF-TRILLION DOLLARS TO INVESTORS TO *PURCHASE* THOSE SO-CALLED "TOXIC ASSETS" AT ARTIFICIALLY INFLATED PRICES--WHILE PROMISING TO COVER ANY *LOSSES* THEY MIGHT INCUR!

AND THEN THE BANKS WILL RESUME LENDING, THE ECONOMY WILL REVIVE, AND EVERYBODY LIVES HAPPILY EVER AFTER!

IT'S ELEGANT IN ITS NON-SIMPLICITY!

Panel 3:

RIGHT-WING NUTJOBS SEE THE PLAN AS FURTHER PROOF THAT OBAMA IS A *SOCIALIST*.

DO YOU KNOW WHAT IT'S CALLED WHEN THE GOVERNMENT BENDS OVER BACKWARDS TO FUND PRIVATE INVESTORS AND AVOID THE SLIGHTEST HINT OF NATIONALIZATION?

IT'S CALLED *NATIONALIZATION*! JUST LIKE WHAT *HITLER* AND *STALIN* DID!

THE PRESIDENT IS A *COMMUNOFASCIST*!

Panel 4:

BUT UNSURPRISINGLY, WALL STREET *LIKES* THE IDEA!

THE MARKET REACTED *VERY FAVORABLY* TO GEITHNER'S PLAN TO POUR HUNDREDS OF BILLIONS OF DOLLARS INTO THE MARKET!

AND *THAT'S* GOOD NEWS-- FOR THE *MARKET*!

Action McNews Network

Panel 5:

AND ALTHOUGH TAXPAYERS WILL CLEARLY END UP FOOTING THE BILL FOR THIS SCHEME--

WE ARE holdIng YOUR eConomy hoStage pAy NOW IF YOU eVER wAnt to SEE Your 401-k agAin

Panel 6:

--YOU SHOULDN'T EXPECT THE SAME RULES TO APPLY TO YOU.

HELLO! WHERE DO I GO TO SIGN UP FOR *MY* EXTREMELY LARGE, ENTIRELY RISK-FREE LOAN?

SORRY--*YOU'RE* NOT TOO BIG TO FAIL. NOW GET OUT OF HERE BEFORE I CALL ANIMAL CONTROL.

TOM TOMORROW©2009

THIS MODERN WORLD

BY TOM TOMORROW

IN THE YEAR OF OUR LORD 2003, I COMPLETED WORK ON MY *TIME MACHINE*...AND AFTER SEVERAL SHORTER JOURNEYS, I SWALLOWED MY TREPIDATION AND SET MY DEVICE TO TRAVEL *SIX YEARS* INTO THE FUTURE...

I SECURED MY CONVEYANCE AND SET OUT CAUTIOUSLY...BUT TO MY SURPRISE, THE FUTURE DWELLERS PAID ME LITTLE NOTICE--AND EVEN ACCEPTED MY ANTIQUATED COINAGE WITHOUT QUESTION...

HAH! WHATEVER ELSE CHANGES, AT LEAST *NEWSPAPERS* WILL NEVER GO OUT OF STYLE! DON'T YOU AGREE, SHOPKEEPER?

WHATEVER YOU SAY, PAL. 75 CENTS, PLEASE.

BUT AS I PERUSED THE BROADSHEET, I BEGAN TO REALIZE WITH DAWNING HORROR THAT I HAD LANDED IN A WORLD GONE *MAD*!

PRESIDENT "OBAMA"?

GAY MARRIAGE LEGAL--IN *IOWA*?

G.O.P. ON THE VERGE OF *COLLAPSE*?

CAPTAIN KIRK AND MR. SPOCK PLAYED BY *NEW ACTORS*?

MY HEART RACING, I SOUGHT REASSURANCE FROM A RANDOM PASSER-BY...AND THEN ANOTHER, UNTIL I CHANCED UPON ONE WITH THE PATIENCE TO *HUMOR* ME...

PRAY TELL, KIND SIR--IS THERE *NO TRACE* LEFT OF THE WORLD OF 2003?

WHAT IS THIS, A CONTEST OR SOMETHING? LET'S SEE--WE *ARE* STILL BOGGED DOWN IN IRAQ AND AFGHANISTAN...

AS HE SPOKE, HIS WORDS FILLED MY VERY HEART WITH *JOY*...

OBAMA'S ADVOCATING HIS OWN VERSION OF *INDEFINITE DETENTION*...NOT TO MENTION EXTRA-JUDICIAL *TRIBUNALS*...THE MILITARY JUST DISMISSED ANOTHER ARABIC TRANSLATOR FOR BEING *GAY*...

BLESS YOU, GOOD SIR! MY WORLD *HASN'T* DISAPPEARED ENTIRELY!

UH, SURE. DID I *WIN*?

BUT MY HAPPINESS WAS SHORT-LIVED... FOR I HAD FORGOTTEN TO SET THE TEMPORAL LOCK ON MY TIME MACHINE! IT HAD RETURNED TO 2003 *WITHOUT* ME--LEAVING ME STRANDED IN A WORLD I COULD STILL BARELY *COMPREHEND*...

EXCUSE ME--WHAT IS THE MEANING OF THIS PHRASE, "SUBPRIME MELTDOWN"? HAS MISFORTUNE SOMEHOW BEFALLEN OUR *ECONOMY*?

HA HA HA! WHAT YEAR ARE YOU *FROM*, DUDE?

EPIC FAIL!

TOM TOMORROW ©2009

42

THIS MODERN WORLD

by TOM TOMORROW

Panel 1:
HELLO! I'M HERE FOR THE TEA PARTY! I'LL HAVE A CUP OF EARL GREY, PLEASE!

WE DON'T *DRINK* THE TEA! WE TEAR THE LITTLE PACKETS OPEN AND DUMP THEIR CONTENTS INTO THE NEAREST BODY OF WATER--THUS STRIKING A BLOW AGAINST *TYRANNY!*

Panel 2:
NO KIDDING! REMIND ME, WHO'S BEING TYRANNIZED, AGAIN?

THE *AMERICAN PEOPLE,* OF COURSE! WHY--DID YOU KNOW THAT OBAMA IS THREATENING TO OPPRESS US ALL WITH A *MASSIVE TAX INCREASE?*

Panel 3:
YOU MEAN HOW HE'S GOING TO LET THE BUSH TAX CUTS FOR THE WEALTHIEST FIVE PERCENT OF AMERICANS *EXPIRE?*

EXACTLY! AND WHAT ABOUT HIS ATTEMPT TO TAKE OVER THE *AUTOMOBILE INDUSTRY?* WHAT DOES *HE* KNOW ABOUT RUNNING A BUSINESS, ANYWAY?

LESS THAN THE CEO'S WHO RAN THEIR COMPANIES INTO THE GROUND, I'LL BET!

Panel 4:
WELL, I'LL TELL YOU--*WE'RE* NOT GOING TO STAND IDLY BY WHILE THE GOVERNMENT TRIES TO DICTATE *TERMS AND CONDITIONS* TO CORPORATIONS JUST BECAUSE IT HAPPENS TO BE BAILING THEM OUT! THAT'S--THAT'S *FASCISM!*

UH--I'M NOT SURE--

Panel 5:
AND--GOSH DARN IT--I JUST--*SOB*--I JUST *LOVE* THIS COUNTRY TOO MUCH TO LET THAT HAPPEN! SNIFFLE! YOU'VE GOT TO BELIEVE IN SOMETHING--*SOB*--EVEN IF IT'S *WRONG!* BOO HOO *HOOO!*

NOW *LEAVE BRITNEY ALONE!!!*

ER, I MEAN AMERICA. LEAVE AMERICA ALONE.

Panel 6:
NOW IF YOU'LL EXCUSE ME--MY FELLOW *TEABAGGERS* AND I... HAVE SOME *TEABAGGING* TO DO!

UM, YOU KNOW--

OH, NEVER MIND.

WE'RE GONNA TEABAG *THEM* BEFORE THEY TEABAG *US!*

Get A BRAIN! MORANS

THIS MODERN WORLD

by TOM TOMORROW

WHAT WE TALK ABOUT WHEN WE TALK ABOUT TORTURE

NOW THAT THE BUSH TORTURE MEMOS HAVE BEEN RELEASED, SENSIBLE CENTRISTS AGREE--IT'S TIME TO *FORGET* ABOUT THE *WHOLE THING!*

IT IS TIME TO MOVE *FORWARD* RATHER THAN *BACKWARD!*

MISTAKES WERE MADE, BUT THAT'S ALL *BEHIND* US NOW--

--AND *THAT* IS A DIRECTION IN WHICH IT IS *NOT* TIME TO MOVE!

?

THE ARCHITECTS OF THAT POLICY MAY SOMEDAY FACE AN INQUIRY... BUT THE PRESIDENT OPPOSES THE PROSECUTION OF ANYONE WHO TORTURED DETAINEES IN "GOOD FAITH"..

AND RIGHTLY *SO!* AFTER ALL--THEY WERE *JUST FOLLOWING ORDERS!*

YOU CERTAINLY CAN'T PROSECUTE ANYONE WHO WAS *JUST FOLLOWING ORDERS!*

YOU KNOW, I'M NOT EVEN GONNA TAKE THE BAIT.

MANY CONSERVATIVES DENY THAT THE BARBARIC TREATMENT DETAILED IN THESE MEMOS (AND ELSEWHERE) CONSTITUTES TORTURE AT *ALL*...

HAR HAR! ANYONE WHO COULD BE WATERBOARDED SIX TIMES A DAY MUST HAVE BEEN *ENJOYING* IT!

YOU WANNA KNOW WHAT'S *REALLY* TORTURE? LISTENING TO NANCY PELOSI ON THE *NEWS!* HA HA!

HA HA! NOT TO MENTION *RAP MUSIC!*

YET AT THE SAME TIME, DICK CHENEY SAYS THE RELEASE OF THE MEMOS HAS PUT OUR COUNTRY IN *DANGER!*

NOW THE TERRORISTS KNOW EXACTLY WHAT TORTURE METHODS WE MIGHT USE ON THEM! OR *NOT* USE!

OR THAT THEY HAVE NOTHING TO FEAR BUT SOME HARMLESS FRATERNITY-STYLE *PRANKS!*

ALL I KNOW IS, *I'M* TERRIFIED!

ONE THING'S FOR SURE--AMERICANS MUST NOW GRAPPLE WITH SOME *EXTREMELY* PERPLEXING ETHICAL DILEMMAS...

CAN HANDCUFFING A PRISONER TO THE CEILING FOR DAYS ON END UNTIL HIS ANKLES AND FEET SWELL TO TWICE THEIR NORMAL CIRCUMFERENCE AND HIS LEGS ARE COVERED WITH WATERY BLISTERS...*REALLY* BE CONSIDERED *TORTURE*?

HECK IF *I* KNOW!

YA GOT *ME!*

ANYTHING GOOD ON TV TONIGHT?

TOM TOMORROW©2009

THIS MODERN WORLD

by TOM TOMORROW

45

THIS MODERN WORLD

by TOM TOMORROW

MISTER VICE PRESIDENT, SHOULD AMERICANS BE **WORRIED** ABOUT THE SWINE FLU?

WORRIED? HELL, THEY SHOULD BE FRIGHTENED OUT OF THEIR **GOURDS**!

I TELL YA, **I** SURE WOULDN'T WANT TO BE FLYING ON A PLANE, OR RIDING ON A SUBWAY--OR **SHOPPING**, FOR THAT MATTER! DO YOU KNOW HOW MANY **GERMS** THERE ARE ON AN AVERAGE DOLLAR BILL?

YOU GO OUT TO THE MALL, YOU MIGHT AS WELL SIGN YOUR OWN **DEATH WARRANT**!

LET'S FACE IT--WE DON'T KNOW HOW VIRULENT THIS FLU **IS** YET, OR HOW TERRIBLE A TOLL IT MAY EXACT! CHRIST JESUS, FOR ALL WE KNOW, THIS IS THE BIG ONE--THE VIRUS THAT TURNS EVERYBODY INTO BRAIN-EATING **ZOMBIES**! IT'S JUST TOO SOON TO **KNOW** FOR SURE!

PROBABLY, YOUR BEST BET IS TO BOARD UP THE DOORS AND WINDOWS ON YOUR HOUSE AND HOLE UP INSIDE WITH A SHOTGUN AND PLENTY OF **AMMO**! I MEAN-- IF YOU'RE STANDING IN A FIELD AND SOMEBODY SNEEZES, THAT'S ONE THING! BUT IF YOU'RE STANDING IN A FIELD FULL OF **BRAIN-EATING ZOMBIES**--

EX-CUSE ME, SIR--

PSSSST PSSST PSSST PRESIDENT OBAMA PSSST PSSST PSSST IXNAY ON THE OMBIEZAYS PSSST PSSSST WIDESPREAD PANIC PSSST PSSST--

OH! OH, RIGHT!

HEH HEH! JUST TO **CLARIFY** MY PREVIOUS STATEMENTS--EVERYTHING IS UNDER CONTROL AND THERE'S NO CAUSE FOR ALARM.

NOW IF YOU'LL EXCUSE ME, I NEED TO GO BOARD UP MY HOUSE.

WHAT? I'M **KID-DING**!

SORT OF.

TOM TOMORROW©2009

THIS MODERN WORLD

by TOM TOMORROW

WELCOME TO THE INCREDIBLE SHRINKING RIGHT-WINGO-VERSE!

THE SMALLER IT GETS-- THE CRAZIER IT GETS!

IN THE RIGHTWINGOVERSE, OBAMA'S USE OF A TELEPROMPTER MAKES HIM A *LAUGHINGSTOCK.*

WHAT A BUFFOON! WHOEVER HEARD OF A PRESIDENT *DOING* SUCH A THING?

IF HE WERE AS MENTALLY AGILE AS HIS *PREDECESSOR*, HE'D HAVE NO *NEED* FOR SUCH A DEVICE!

IN THE RIGHTWINGOVERSE, THE RESPECTED DEAN OF THE YALE LAW SCHOOL WANTS TO USE HIS NEW POST AT THE STATE DEPARTMENT TO IMPOSE *SHARIAH LAW!*

I KNOW IT'S TRUE--BECAUSE I READ A STORY IN THE NEW YORK POST BASED ON AN ANEDCOTAL ACCOUNT OF A REMARK HE SUPPOSEDLY MADE AT SOME *PARTY!* *

WELL, IT DOESN'T GET ANY MORE CREDIBLE THAN *THAT!*

*ACTUAL SOURCE OF RUMOR.

IN THE RIGHTWINGOVERSE, IT IS AN ACCEPTED JOURNALISTIC PRACTICE TO HARASS COLLEGE PROFESSORS ON THE STREET.

HEY PROFESSOR SMARTYPANTS! YA WROTE SOMETHIN' KINDA *LIBERAL* SOUNDING IN YER FANCYPANTS *TEXTBOOK!* WHAT ARE YA, A *COMMIE?* HUH? HUH? WHATSAMATTER, *CAT* GOT YER TONGUE?

HUH?

HUH?

FOX "NEWS" EGGHEAD PROF WROTE SOMETHING WE DIDN'T LIKE

IN THE RIGHTWINGOVERSE, THE PRESIDENT IS AS *SUBMISSIVE* ABROAD AS HE IS *DOMINEERING* AT HOME!

WHEN HE'S NOT BUSY SIGNALLING HIS INTENTION TO SURRENDER TO THE *TALIBAN*--

--HE'S PLOTTING TO TAKE OUR *GUNS* AWAY!

WHAT A *WUSS* AND/OR *TYRANT!*

IN THE RIGHTWINGOVERSE, *TRUE* PATRIOTS LOVE AMERICA SO MUCH, THEY'RE READY TO *SECEDE!*

IT'S BEEN *THREE ENTIRE MONTHS* SINCE OBAMA TOOK OFFICE--AND I'VE BEEN DRIVEN TO THE *BRINK* BY THE POLICIES HE IS ENACTING IN MY IMAGINATION!

WE MIGHT NEED TO *DESTROY* THIS COUNTRY--IN ORDER TO *SAVE* IT!

U.S.A!! U.S.A!!

Get A BRAIN! MORANS

TOM TOMORROW©2009

47

THIS MODERN WORLD

by TOM TOMORROW

Panel 1

HELLO, MOONBAT! YOU'RE JUST IN TIME! MY COLLEAGUE IN DETECTION, **GLENN BECK**, HAS BROUGHT A **MYSTERY** TO MY ATTENTION!

GREAT. SAY, HAVE YOU BEEN GETTING OUT MUCH? YOU LOOK **PALE**...

OH, MOONBAT! HOW **WILL** I DISPOSE OF YOUR BODY, WHEN I CAN FINALLY STAND YOUR NONSENSICAL BABBLING NO **LONGER**?

ER--WHAT?

Panel 2

FOCUS, MOONBAT! THERE ARE SINISTER FORCES AT WORK--AS I'LL EXPLAIN, IF I CAN BRIEFLY SUBDUE THE FLUTTERING SONGBIRD OF YOUR **ATTENTION**! BUT FIRST-- CAN YOU IDENTIFY THIS **SYMBOL**?

I-- UH--

IT IS THE ANCIENT ROMAN **FASCES**--A SYMBOL OF AUTHORITY CO-OPTED IN THE EARLY 20TH CENTURY BY THE ITALIAN **FASCISTS**!

Panel 3

NOW LOOK AT THE BACK OF THIS MERCURY DIME--WHICH, AS MISTER BECK POINTS OUT, WAS MINTED DURING THE ADMINISTRATION OF **WOODROW WILSON**--AND WHAT DO YOU **SEE**? THE **SYMBOL OF FASCISM**, THAT'S WHAT!

IT'S PROOF, MOONBAT--HISTORICAL PROOF THAT **DEMOCRATS ARE FASCISTS**!

UM, CAN I USE YOUR COMPUTER?

Panel 4

OF COURSE! I SUPPOSE YOU CAN'T WAIT TO ALERT YOUR SOCIAL NETWORKING FRIENDS TO THIS **STUNNING DISCOVERY**! I'D DO THE SAME, IF MY DETECTING DUTIES LEFT TIME FOR SUCH FRIVOLITIES!

ACTUALLY, USING A SOPHISTICATED DETECTIVE TOOL I CALL "GOOGLE," **I** HAVE JUST LEARNED--

Panel 5

--THAT THE MERCURY DIME **PREDATES** THE BIRTH OF FASCISM BY SEVERAL **YEARS**...AND THAT THE SYMBOL OF THE **FASCES** CAN ALSO BE FOUND IN THE **OVAL OFFICE**, IN THE **HOUSE OF REPRESENTATIVES**, AND ON THE **LINCOLN MEMORIAL**-- JUST TO NAME A **FEW**!

GOOD **GOD**, MOONBAT--DO YOU KNOW WHAT THIS **MEANS**?

Panel 6

THAT GLENN BECK IS AN IDIOT?

THAT THE FASCISTS HAVE BEEN TRYING TO TAKE OVER THIS COUNTRY-- SINCE BEFORE THEY EVEN **EXISTED**!

OF COURSE. SILLY ME.

NOW IF YOU'LL EXCUSE ME-- THE **GAME'S AFOOT**!

NEXT: THE TIME TRAVELLING FASCIST DEMOCRAT CONSPIRACY TO IMPOSE SHARIA LAW ON THE U.S.--**EXPOSED**!

TOM TOMORROW©2009

THIS MODERN WORLD

by TOM TOMORROW

I'M IMPRESSED, BIFF! REPUBLICANS ARE OUT OF POWER AND ALMOST UNIVERSALLY LOATHED--BUT WHEN IT COMES TO **NATIONAL SE-CURITY**, SOMEHOW YOU **STILL** MANAGE TO SET THE TERMS OF THE DEBATE!

OBAMA'S CERTAINLY PLAYING BY YOUR RULES--HE'S ACTUALLY HELPING **COVER UP** THE CRIMES OF THE BUSH ADMINISTRATION!

HE'S WITHHOLDING INFORMATION ON TORTURE AND RENDITION-- AND PRESSURING THE **BRITISH** GOVERNMENT TO DO THE **SAME**--

--HE'S SIDING WITH BUSH'S JUSTICE DEPARTMENT ON THE SECRECY OF WARRANTLESS WIRETAPPING--HE'S OPPOSED TO WAR CRIMES PROSE-CUTIONS, THOUGH IT SHOULDN'T EVEN **BE** HIS DECISION--

--AND NOW HE'S DONE A 180 ON RELEASING THE LASTEST BATCH OF **TORTURE** PHOTOS! HE'S MADE IT CLEAR--WE'RE NOT GOING TO FACE UP TO THE DETAILS OF WHAT WAS DONE IN AMERICA'S NAME! WE'RE GOING TO SWEEP IT ALL UNDER THE RUG AND POLITELY PRETEND IT NEVER **HAPPENED**!

IT'S ASTONISHING! I MEAN, HOW DOES ONE OF THE MOST POPULAR PRESIDENTS IN HISTORY END UP EFFECTIVELY CEDING THIS ARGU-MENT TO **DICK CHENEY**?

I HONESTLY DON'T KNOW HOW YOU GUYS **DO** IT--

OBAMA IS A SOCIALIST **FASCIST** WHO IS SECRETLY PLOTTING THE DOWNFALL OF WESTERN CIVILIZATION.

--ESPECIALLY CON-SIDERING THAT YOU'RE QUITE LITERALLY **INSANE**.

AND HEALTH CARE REFORM IS THE FIRST STEP TOWARD **ONE WORLD GOVERNMENT**!

SERIOUSLY, I'M IN AWE.

THIS MODERN WORLD

by TOM TOMORROW

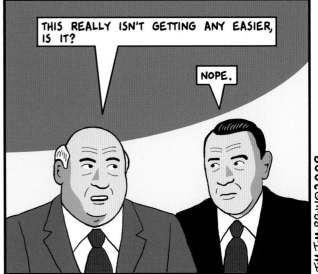

THIS MODERN WORLD

by TOM TOMORROW

Panel 1:
BACK IN THE EARLY DAYS OF THE IRAQ WAR, RIGHT WING BLOGGERS PROCLAIMED THEMSELVES AN IMPORTANT PART OF THE ACTION.

WE'RE FIGHTING A WAR *TOO*-- A WAR OF *IDEAS!*

OUR BATTLE-GROUND IS THE *INTER-NET!*

IT'S *JUST LIKE* BEING DEPLOYED, EXCEPT WE'RE AT HOME, AND NOT BEING SHOT AT.

Panel 2:
TODAY, MANY BLOGGERS ARE PLAYING AN *EQUALLY* IMPORTANT ROLE IN THE IRANIAN PROTESTS!

WE'RE HELPING THE DEMONSTRATORS--BY CHANGING OUR BLOG TEMPLATES TO PROMINENTLY FEATURE THE COLOR *GREEN!*

IT'S LIKE WE'RE PART OF THE UPRISING, EXCEPT WE'RE AT HOME, AND NOT IRANIAN!

Panel 3:
MEANWHILE, CONSERVATIVES WANT TO KNOW WHY *OBAMA* HASN'T INSERTED HIMSELF MORE FORCEFULLY INTO THE IRANIAN SITUATION!

WHERE IS HIS SOLIDARITY WITH THE FREEDOM-LOVING PEOPLES OF IRAN?

HIS CALLOUS INDIFFERENCE TO THEIR PLIGHT IS *TRULY* APPALLING!

Panel 4:
OF COURSE, IT WASN'T SO LONG AGO THAT MANY OF THESE SAME CONSERVATIVES WERE OPENLY ADVOCATING MASS, INDISCRIMINATE *DEATH* FOR IRANIANS...

BOMB BOMB BOMB, BOMB BOMB *IRAN*...HEH HEH HEH...

(IN SOME ALTERNATE UNIVERSE, THIS MAN IS *PRESIDENT*...)

Panel 5:
AND MORE TO THE POINT--WHAT COULD *POSSIBLY* BE MORE HELPFUL TO IRANIAN PROTESTERS THAN A STRONG SHOW OF SUPPORT FROM THE *AMERICAN GOVERNMENT?*

WHY--I DID NOT *REALIZE* THAT OUR AMERICAN FRIENDS THINK THAT IT'S TIME FOR HARDLINERS SUCH AS OURSELVES TO STEP ASIDE!

WHY DID SOMEONE NOT TELL US *SOONER?*

Panel 6:
BUT IN FAIRNESS, IT SHOULD BE ACKNOWLEDGED THAT THE AMERICAN RIGHT *DOES* HAVE A HISTORY OF PROTESTING STOLEN ELECTIONS...

HEY HEY! HO HO! HANGING CHADS HAVE GOT TO *GO!*

TWO FOUR SIX EIGHT! STOP THE RECOUNT OR WE'LL *LITIGATE!*

...PROTESTING IN *FAVOR* OF THEM, THAT IS...

TOM TOMORROW©2009

THIS MODERN WORLD

by TOM TOMORROW

HERE WE GO AGAIN

1) DEMOCRATS PROPOSE HALF-ASSED HEALTH CARE REFORM.

THE "PUBLIC OPTION" PROVIDES AN **ALTERNATIVE** TO PRIVATE INSURANCE--BUT DOES NOT **REPLACE** IT!

THERE'S NO **WAY** OUR OPPONENTS CAN DEMONIZE **THIS** PLAN AS SOCIALIZED MEDICINE!

2) OPPONENTS SWIFTLY DEMONIZE PLAN AS SOCIALIZED MEDICINE.

THEY'RE TRYING TO DESTROY THE **BEST** PATCHWORK SYSTEM OF FOR-PROFIT HEALTH INSURANCE INEXPLICABLY LINKED TO EMPLOYMENT STATUS IN THE **WORLD**!

WHY DO LIBERALS HATE THE FREE MARKET?

3) VOTERS ARE TERRIFIED BY STORIES OF UNCARING BUREAUCRACIES, COMPLICATED PAPERWORK, AND LONG WAITS FOR ROUTINE CARE.

THANK GOODNESS WE DO NOT EXPERIENCE ANY OF THESE THINGS UNDER OUR **PRESENT** SYSTEM!

GREAT NEWS! I GOT AN APPOINTMENT FOR A CHECKUP IN **2011**!

4) IN AN ECONOMY **THIS** BAD, WE ARE TOLD THAT HEALTH CARE REFORM WILL SIMPLY COST MORE THAN WE CAN **AFFORD**!

PROVIDING COVERAGE TO THE UNINSURED IS **IMPORTANT**--BUT NOT AS IMPORTANT AS **BAILING OUT WALL STREET**!

BETTER LUCK **NEXT** TIME--IN **ANOTHER** TWENTY YEARS OR SO!

5) WITH A REPORTED 72% OF AMERICANS STILL IN FAVOR OF REFORM, THE ONLY **REAL** QUESTION IS...HOW WILL DEMOCRATS BLOW IT **THIS** TIME?

IN THE SPIRIT OF BIPARTISAN CO-OPERATION, WE'VE **ELIMINATED** THE "PUBLIC OPTION"! OUR **NEW** PLAN PROVIDES EVERY AMERICAN WITH A **BAND-AID** AND A BOTTLE OF **ASPIRIN**!

WHOA! WHAT IS THIS-- **SOVIET RUSSIA**?

THIS MODERN WORLD

by TOM TOMORROW

DICK CHENEY MAKES A STARTLING ADMISSION!

OH, SURE, I'VE KILLED *LOTS* OF PEOPLE! USED TO HUNT THEM FOR SPORT ON THE SOUTH LAWN!

MAN *IS* THE MOST DANGEROUS GAME, YOU KNOW!

A FURIOUS *DEBATE* ERUPTS!

THE LAW IS THE *LAW!* IF THE FORMER VICE PRESIDENT HUNTED HUMAN BEINGS LIKE ANIMALS, HE SHOULD BE PUT ON *TRIAL--* ALONG WITH ANYONE WHO HELPED HIM GET *AWAY* WITH IT!

OH COME *ON!* THE *LAST* THING THIS COUNTRY NEEDS RIGHT NOW IS A *PARTISAN WITCH HUNT!*

CONGRESSIONAL DEMOCRATS TRY TO *FINESSE* THE ISSUE!

WHAT THE FORMER VICE-PRESIDENT DID WAS *CLEARLY* WRONG! BUT WHY WASTE TIME WITH A DIVISIVE, PROLONGED *PROSECUTION*--WHEN A FIRMLY WORDED *DENUNCIATION* WILL DO?

BAD MISTER CHENEY! VERY, VERY *BAD!*

PRESIDENT OBAMA ISSUES A MEASURED STATEMENT OF *DISAPPROVAL*--

RATHER LARGE, UH, ERRORS IN JUDGEMENT WERE MADE--BUT THAT'S ALL *BEHIND* US NOW!

--AND MAKES A SMALL JOKE--

JUST WATCH YOUR BACK AROUND CHENEY! HEH HEH HEH!

--WHICH TALK RADIO HOSTS IMMEDIATELY SEIZE UPON AS THE *REAL* OUTRAGE!

IT'S INCREDIBLE! HOW *DARE* HE EXPRESS SUCH CONTEMPT FOR THE HALLOWED OFFICE OF THE VICE PRESIDENT OF THE UNITED STATES!

SOB! I--I CAN'T *BELIEVE* THAT THE PRESIDENT WOULD TREAT A DEVOTED PUBLIC SERVANT LIKE MISTER CHENEY WITH SUCH CASUAL DISRESPECT!

AND FINALLY, A *CENTRIST* CONSENSUS EMERGES.

SURE, HUNTING HUMAN BEINGS WAS CLEARLY A *MISTAKE*--BUT DIDN'T WE *ALL* GO A LITTLE CRAZY AFTER 9/11?

AND CHENEY *WAS* UNDER A LOT OF PRESSURE!

IT WOULDN'T BE *FAIR* TO GO BACK AND SECOND-GUESS HIM *NOW!*

NEXT: IS CANNIBALISM *REALLY* SO WRONG?

TOM TOMORROW©2009

THIS MODERN WORLD

by TOM TOMORROW

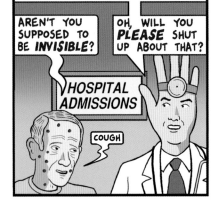

THIS WEEK: HEALTH CARE AND THE FREE MARKET--WITH YOUR HOST, *DOCTOR HAND!*

I'M NOT *REALLY* A DOCTOR, BUT I DRESS LIKE ONE--SO AS TO APPEAR IMPLICITLY *TRUSTWORTHY!*

AREN'T YOU SUPPOSED TO BE *INVISIBLE?*

OH, WILL YOU *PLEASE* SHUT UP ABOUT THAT?

HOSPITAL ADMISSIONS

COUGH

SPEAKING AS SOMEONE DRESSED LIKE A DOCTOR, I MUST SAY-- YOU'RE NOT LOOKING VERY WELL! LET'S TAKE A CLOSER LOOK--AT YOUR *WALLET!*

AH, WE'RE IN *LUCK!* YOU SEEM TO BE *INSURED!*

SO CAN I SEE A REAL DOCTOR NOW?

HOSPITAL ADMISSIONS

YOU KNOW, IT'S INTERESTING...SOME PEOPLE THINK INSURANCE SHOULD BE A WAY OF POOLING SOCIETY'S RESOURCES, SO THAT THOSE WHO FALL *ILL* CAN RECEIVE THE CARE THEY *NEED.*

OF COURSE, THAT WOULD BE *SO-CIALISM*--AND WE CERTAINLY CAN'T HAVE *THAT!*

COUGH COUGH

HOSPITAL ADMISSIONS

FORTUNATELY THE GENIUS OF THE *FREE MARKET* HAS GIVEN US A SYSTEM OF *PRIVATE* INSURERS, COMMITTED FIRST AND FOREMOST TO HEALTHY *PROFITS*--AND HEY, SPEAKING OF THE *DEVIL*--

HELLO! I'M FROM THE INSURANCE COMPANY--AND THIS MUST BE THE LIABILITY--ER, THE *PATIENT!*

YES--I DON'T KNOW WHAT'S WRONG WITH HIM...BUT IT LOOKS *EXPENSIVE!*

HOSPITAL ADMISSIONS

HMM--WHAT'S *THIS?* IT LOOKS LIKE YOU DIDN'T TELL US ABOUT A TRIP TO THE *PODIATRIST* IN 1986! THAT MEANS *ANYTHING* WRONG WITH YOU CAN BE CON-SIDERED A *PRE-EXISTING CONDITION*--AND *THAT* MEANS WE'RE CANCELLING YOUR COVERAGE!

BEST OF LUCK! DON'T LET THE DOOR HIT YOU ON THE WAY OUT!

HOSPITAL ADMISSIONS

WHAT?

AND THERE YOU HAVE IT, FOLKS! IT'S ANOTHER SUCCESS STORY FOR THE PRIME BENEFICIARY OF OUR HEALTH CARE SYSTEM--THE *AMER-ICAN INSURANCE INDUSTRY!*

WE'RE HERE TO HELP *YOU* HELP *US!*

NOW LET'S GET OUT OF HERE! ALL THESE SICK PEOPLE--IT'S *SO* DEPRESSING!

BUT-- BUT--

HOSPITAL ADMISSIONS

TOM TOMORROW©2009

THIS MODERN WORLD

by TOM TOMORROW

Panel 1: IT'S MADDENINGLY SIMPLE--IF YOU WANT TO SAVE MONEY *AND* COVER EVERYONE, TAKE THE PROFIT MOTIVE OUT OF THE *INSURANCE* SYSTEM.

MY 17-YEAR-OLD DAUGHTER NEEDS A NEW LIVER OR SHE'LL *DIE!*

SIR--IF WE PAY FOR A NEW LIVER FOR EVERY TEENAGER WHO GETS A *SNIFFLE*, HOW WILL WE AFFORD OUR CEO'S $13 MILLION *SALARY?*

BUH-BYE NOW.

(BASED ON TRUE, TRAGIC STORY--GIRL DIED.)

Panel 2: AS OBAMA HIMSELF ACKNOWLEDGED IN HIS RECENT PRESS CONFERENCE:

"THE TRUTH IS THAT UNLESS YOU HAVE WHAT'S CALLED THE SINGLE PAYER SYSTEM IN WHICH EVERY-BODY'S AUTOMATICALLY COVERED, YOU'RE PROBABLY NOT GOING TO REACH EVERY SINGLE INDIVIDUAL..."

Panel 3: SO OF COURSE SINGLE PAYER'S NOT EVEN ON THE TABLE...THE BEST WE CAN HOPE FOR IS A "PUBLIC OPTION"... WHICH, AS IT TURNS OUT, MAY NOT COVER ABORTION...

I CERTAINLY DON'T WANT *MY* TAX DOLLARS TO BE USED FOR SOME-THING I *OPPOSE!*

GOSH, WHAT A GOOD POINT! NOW LET'S TALK ABOUT THE *IRAQ WAR*, *GUANTANAMO*, AND THE *GOLDMAN SACHS BAILOUTS!*

FOR START-ERS.

Panel 4: THIS HASN'T STOPPED CONSERVATIVES FROM CAMPAIGNING *AGAINST* A SINGLE-PAYER SYSTEM...WHICH THE IMAGINARY OBAMA WHO LIVES IN THEIR *HEADS* HAS APPARENTLY PROPOSED...

HE WANTS TO TURN THIS COUNTRY INTO A TOTALITARIAN *NIGHTMARE*-- JUST LIKE *CANADA!*

YOUR GRAND-PARENTS WILL BE EUTHANIZED-- EVEN IF THEY'RE NOT *SICK!*

THE STARS ON OUR FLAG WILL BE REPLACED-- WITH *MAPLE LEAVES!*

Panel 5: THE TRULY PUZZLING THING IS-- WHO *ARE* THESE PEOPLE, WHO ARE SO ENAMORED OF OUR HEALTH CARE SYSTEM AS IT PRESENTLY EXISTS?

I *LOVE* HAVING MY HEALTH CARE DECISIONS MADE BY INSURANCE COMPANY *ACCOUNTANTS!*

I'M HOOKED ON THE DEATH-DEFYING THRILL I GET FROM KNOWING THAT MY COVERAGE COULD BE CANCELLED AT A *MOMENT'S NOTICE!*

Panel 6: IT'S ALL ENOUGH TO MAKE YOUR HEAD EXPLODE--BUT YOU'D BETTER CHECK WITH YOUR INSURANCE COM-PANY *FIRST*...

I'M SORRY, SIR--EXPLODING HEADS ARE NOT COVERED UNDER THE TERMS OF YOUR POLICY.

ON THE BRIGHT SIDE--AT LEAST YOU'RE FREE FROM THE *TYRANNY* OF *GUARANTEED HEALTH CARE!*

URK.

BUH-BYE NOW.

TOM TOMORROW©2009

55

THIS MODERN WORLD

by TOM TOMORROW

MORE TO THE PICTURE

RIGHT-WINGERS HAD A FIELD DAY RECENTLY WITH A PHOTO THAT SEEMED TO SHOW OBAMA CHECKING OUT A YOUNG WOMAN'S BUTT-- EVEN THOUGH THE VIDEO MADE IT CLEAR HE **WASN'T**...

BUT THAT WASN'T THE **ONLY** POTENTIALLY MISLEADING PHOTO RELEASED IN RECENT DAYS!

FOR INSTANCE, IN THIS NEVER-BE-FORE-SEEN SHOT FROM 2003, DICK CHENEY **APPEARS** TO GLOWER MALEVOLENTLY AS HE THINKS UP NEW WAYS TO UNDERMINE THE FUNDAMENTAL PRINCIPLES WHICH DEFINE US AS A **DEMOCRACY!**

IN REALITY--THAT'S WHAT HE **ALWAYS** LOOKS LIKE!

AND IN **THIS** PHOTO, WILLIAM KRISTOL **SEEMS** TO BE CONTEMPLATING THE SHEER OVERWHELMING WRONGNESS OF EVERY PUBLIC PRONOUNCEMENT HE'S EVER **MADE!**

ACTUALLY HE WAS JUST CHECKING OUT A YOUNG WOMAN'S BUTT!

AND--LOOKING AT THIS SHOT OF THE CEO OF GOLDMAN SACHS, YOU MIGHT **THINK** HE WAS CHUCKLING GLEEFULLY AT THE THOUGHT OF ANNOUNCING A $1.8 BILLION PROFIT WHILE BENEFITTING FROM MORE THAN $40 BILLION IN TAX-PAYER SUBSIDIES (**NOT** INCLUDING THE REPAID **TARP** FUNDS)!

IN THIS CASE YOU'D BE RIGHT!

AS FOR **THIS** PICTURE, IN WHICH SPARKY THE PENGUIN SEEMS TO HAVE BEEN CAUGHT IN SOME SORT OF SCANDALOUS ACT INVOLVING REGIS PHILBIN, A CIRCUS CONTORTIONIST, AND SEVERAL LINGERIE MODELS--

--WE HAVE NO COMMENT AT THIS TIME...

THIS MODERN WORLD

by TOM TOMORROW

Panel 1:

IN THE RIGHTWINGOVERSE, ABORTION IS A CHOICE MADE CASUALLY BY CALLOUS LIBERTINES.

HEY GIRLS, LET'S GO SHOPPING THIS AFTERNOON--AND THEN GET *ABORTIONS ON DEMAND!*

OKAY, BUT ONLY IF I'VE GOT TIME FOR A PEDICURE AFTER!

DARN IT! I'M NOT EVEN PREGNANT!

Panel 2:

IN THE RIGHTWINGOVERSE, WOMEN WOULD IDEALLY BE TREATED AS BREEDING STOCK.

BUT--BUT--THE DOCTOR SAYS THIS PREGNANCY COULD ENDANGER MY *LIFE!*

SHOULDA THOUGHT OF THAT *BEFORE* YOU HAD YOUR LITTLE FUN, ELSIE!

Panel 3:

IN THE RIGHTWINGOVERSE, ACTS OF TERRORISM COMMITTED BY RELIGIOUS FANATICS ARE SOMETIMES A *GOOD* THING.

WHUT? YOU MEAN OUR ORGANIZED HARASSMENT AND INTIMIDATION OF ABORTION PROVIDERS, UP TO AND INCLUDING MURDER?

HOW CAN *THAT* BE TERRORISM? DO WE LOOK MUSLIM TO *YOU?*

Panel 4:

IN THE RIGHTWINGOVERSE, IT IS APPROPRIATE TO EQUATE A VIOLENT CRIME WITH DENUNCIATIONS *OF* THAT CRIME.

SURE, IT'S WRONG TO KILL DOCTORS, BLAH BLAH BLAH! BUT IT'S *ALSO* WRONG TO *POLITICIZE* SUCH KILLINGS IN ORDER TO DISCREDIT THE PEOPLE WHO *COMMIT* THEM!

HAVE THE LIBERALS NO *SHAME?*

Panel 5:

AND FINALLY...IN THE RIGHTWINGOVERSE, PEOPLE ARE HIGHLY SUSCEPTIBLE TO THE PERNICIOUS INFLUENCE OF VIDEO GAMES, POPULAR MUSIC AND SITUATION COMEDIES--

THAT SHOW WITH THE BUMBLING DAD *COMPLETELY UNDERMINES* MALE PARENTAL AUTHORITY!

AND THE ONE WITH THE HOMOSEXUAL DOES *UNTOLD DAMAGE* TO THE INSTITUTION OF MARRIAGE!

Panel 6:

--BUT ARE IN *NO WAY* AFFECTED BY THE ENDLESSLY-REPEATED RAVINGS OF POPULAR TELEVISION COMMENTATORS.

JUST BECAUSE I SPENT *YEARS* PORTRAYING THE VICTIM AS "TILLER THE BABY KILLER"--YOU THINK I BEAR SOME *RESPONSIBILITY* HERE?

YOU PROBABLY GOT *THAT* IDEA FROM THE HATEFUL DAILY KOS! *THEY* HAVE A LOT OF INFLUENCE!

UN-LIKE *ME!*

NEXT: IN THE RIGHTWINGOVERSE, THERE ARE *TWO SIDES* TO EVERY STORY!

ONE SIDE HAS DERANGED *MURDERERS...*

THE OTHER HAS...*AL FRANKEN!*

TOM TOMORROW©2009

THIS MODERN WORLD

STRANGE DAYS

THIS IS TRUE: GLENN BECK RECENTLY IMPLORED HIS AUDIENCE NOT TO GO ON ANY *KILLING SPREES.*

"JUST ONE LUNATIC LIKE TIMOTHY MCVEIGH COULD RUIN *EVERYTHING!*"

IT'S NOT A REMINDER KEITH OLBERMANN OFTEN GIVES *HIS* AUDIENCE...

"BIRTHERS" CONTINUE TO MAKE FOOLS OF THEMSELVES--MOST RECENTLY, FALLING FOR A BLATANTLY-FORGED KENYAN BIRTH CERTIFICATE...

UM--THIS IS FILLED OUT IN *CRAYON...*

KENYANS ARE VERY *POOR!*

AND THE BABY'S NAME IS "PRESIDENT OBAMA."

THEY'RE ALSO VERY *PRESCIENT!*

AND LET'S NOT FORGET THE LATEST *TEABAGGER* CRAZE--ORGANIZED DISRUPTIONS OF CONGRESSIONAL TOWN HALL MEETINGS...

WE ARE HERE TO DEFEND AMERICA-- FROM THE TERRIFYING SPECTER OF *UNIVERSAL HEALTH CARE!*

OR AT LEAST, MODEST REFORMS IN THAT *GENERAL DIRECTION!*

THE LUNACY'S AT A FEVER PITCH THESE DAYS...APPARENTLY FOR THE FAR RIGHT, THE ELECTION OF OUR FIRST BLACK PRESIDENT HAS BEEN AS TRAUMATIC AS A SECOND 9-11...

OUR COUNTRY IS BEING TAKEN OVER--BY STRANGE *OTHER* PEOPLE WHO ARE NOT LIKE *US* IN THEIR STRANGE MENACING *OTHERNESS!*

WHO DO THEY THINK THEY *ARE*, WINNING AN ELECTION IN *OUR* COUNTRY?

SOME WELL-MEANING SOULS THINK THE BEST WAY TO DEAL WITH THE CRAZIES IS TO *IGNORE* THEM.

IF I STICK MY FINGERS IN MY EARS AND LOOK THE OTHER WAY-- IT'S AS IF THEY DON'T EVEN *EXIST!*

ANYWAY, RIGHT-WINGERS ARE MOMENTARILY OUT OF POWER--SO WHO CARES *WHAT* THEY DO *EVER AGAIN*?

WE'RE NOT SO SURE ABOUT THAT.

LOOK *OUT!* YOU'RE HEADED FOR THAT *CLIFF!**

OH--AND WE'RE BANKRUPT. AND I JUST FOUND OUT I HAVE *CANCER.*

NOT TO *WORRY!* IF WE *IGNORE* OUR PROBLEMS-- THEY'LL ALL JUST *GO AWAY!*

WHEEEEEEE!!!

*ANOTHER IN OUR OCCASIONAL SERIES OF CARTOON METAPHORS INVOLVING CLIFFS.

<figure>TOM TOMORROW©2009</figure>

THIS MODERN WORLD

by TOM TOMORROW

HOPE FOR EVENTUAL CHANGE

HE BEGAN HIS CANDIDACY WITH A CLEAR AND COMPELLING VISION!

I AM RUNNING FOR PRESIDENT BECAUSE OF SOMETHING *I* CALL THE "FIERCE URGENCY OF MAYBE SOMEDAY!"

HIS SOARING CAMPAIGN RHETORIC WAS NOTHING SHORT OF INSPIRATIONAL!

AS PRESIDENT, I WILL FIGHT FOR VAGUE AND UNSPECIFIED REFORMS TO OUR HEALTH CARE SYSTEM, WHICH MIGHT POSSIBLY BE SOME KIND OF IMPROVEMENT. UNLESS THEY'RE NOT.

HIS PROMISES WERE CLEAR AND UNAMBIGUOUS...

AND I WILL *CONSIDER* CLOSING GUANTANAMO -- AS A SYMBOL OF MY COMMITMENT TO, UH, USING SOME *OTHER* FACILITY AS AN EXTRA-LEGAL PRISON INSTEAD!

AND I WILL COME UP WITH LEGAL JUSTI-FICATIONS FOR INDEFINITE DE-TENTION THAT MY PREDECES-SORS NEVER *DREAMED* OF!

...AND SO FAR, HE'S KEPT EVERY *ONE* OF THEM!

I *FURTHER* PLEDGE TO EM-BRACE BUSH'S "STATE SECRETS" POLICY...TO SUPPRESS EVIDENCE OF TORTURE AND BLOCK PROSE-CUTIONS OF SAME...TO SUPPORT THE DEFENSE OF MARRIAGE ACT... *AND* TO HEM AND HAW ON "DON'T ASK, DON'T TELL"!

SO--WHY ON *EARTH* ARE SOME FAR-LEFT WACKOS ALREADY GIVING HIM SUCH A *HARD TIME*?

IT MAKES NO *SENSE*! IT'S AS IF THEY BELIEVE HE MADE ENTIRELY *DIFFERENT* PROMISES!

WHAT PLANET HAVE THEY BEEN *LIVING* ON?

AND WHY CAN'T THEY BE *SEN-SIBLE* ABOUT THINGS--LIKE *WE* ARE?

GO FIGURE!

TOM TOMORROW©2009

THIS MODERN WORLD

by TOM TOMORROW

TOP FIVE REASONS WE DO NOT NEED OBAMA'S PROPOSED CONSUMER FINANCIAL PROTECTION AGENCY

BROUGHT TO YOU BY YOUR GOOD FRIENDS IN THE BANKING INDUSTRY

1) IMPOSE NEW REGULATIONS ON THE BANKING INDUSTRY? WHATEVER *FOR?*

ADMITTEDLY MISTAKES HAVE BEEN *MADE*--BUT THAT'S ALL BEHIND US *NOW!*

YOU HAVE OUR *WORD OF HONOR!*

2) RISK-TAKING WILL BE *DISCOURAGED!*

AND OF COURSE WE REFER TO THE SORT OF "RISK-TAKING" WHICH DOES *NOT* LEAD TO THE NEAR-COLLAPSE OF THE ENTIRE FINANCIAL SYSTEM! HEH HEH!

WE'VE LEARNED OUR LESSON! NOW GET OVER IT ALREADY!

3) INNOVATION WILL BE *STIFLED!*

DREAMERS SUCH AS OURSELVES CANNOT FUNCTION WITH SOME GOVERNMENT BUREAUCRAT WATCHING OUR EVERY *MOVE!*

OUR CREATIVE SPIRITS WILL SIMPLY WITHER AWAY AND *DIE!*

4) IT IS AN INSULT TO *CONSUMERS!*

THE GOVERNMENT DOESN'T THINK YOU'RE *SMART* ENOUGH TO SORT THROUGH OUR SCAMS ON YOUR *OWN!*

AND BY "SCAMS" WE MEAN "EXCITING FINANCIAL OPPORTUNITIES"!

5) AN INJURY TO CREDIT CARD COMPANIES IS AN INJURY TO *ALL!*

AS LONG AS FINANCIAL INSTITUTIONS SUCH AS OURS SUFFER THE INJUSTICE OF NEEDLESS REGULATORY *OVERSIGHT*--

--THEN *NO* MAN OR WOMAN CAN TRULY BE FREE!

TO THE *BARRICADES*, COMRADES!

TOM TOMORROW©2009

THIS MODERN WORLD

by TOM TOMORROW

ONCE UPON A TIME, THE CITIZENS OF A VERY LARGE NATION BEGAN TO TURN INTO MONSTERS.

ABU GHRAIB WAS THE WORK OF A *FEW BAD APPLES!*

ANYWAY, WE'RE AT *WAR!* THESE THINGS *HAPPEN!*

IT HAPPENED SLOWLY, OVER THE COURSE OF EIGHT YEARS OR SO... AND AT FIRST, THEY DIDN'T EVEN REALIZE IT HAD HAPPENED AT *ALL*...

WATERBOARDING ISN'T TORTURE! IT'S MORE LIKE A *HARMLESS FRATERNITY PRANK!*

AS IS SHACKLING PRISONERS TO THE CEILING FOR DAYS ON END UNTIL THEIR FEET SWELL UP TO TWICE THEIR NORMAL SIZE!

BUT AT LEAST SOME OF THEM BEGAN TO NOTICE THAT THEY WERE AVOIDING *MIRRORS*...AND THAT THEIR *NEW* PRESIDENT *ENCOURAGED* THIS AVOIDANCE...

NOW IS NOT THE TIME TO LOOK BACKWARDS--AT WHAT WE *ARE!* NOW IS THE TIME TO LOOK FORWARDS--AT WHAT WE *WISH* WE WERE!

AS TIME WENT BY, THE EVIDENCE OF THEIR MONSTROSITY BECOME INCREASINGLY DIFFICULT TO IGNORE.

--AND APPARENTLY MORE THAN A HUNDRED DETAINEES *DIED* IN CUSTODY...MANY UNDER EXTREMELY QUESTIONABLE CIRCUMSTANCES...

DO YOU *MIND?* I'M *TRYING* TO WATCH JON AND KATE'S DIVORCE LAWYERS ON *"ENTERTAINMENT TONIGHT"!*

THE ATTORNEY GENERAL OF THE VERY LARGE NATION BEGAN TO SUGGEST THAT CITIZENS SHOULD AT LEAST TAKE A *QUICK* LOOK AT THEMSELVES.

YOU DON'T HAVE TO LOOK IN A FULL-LENGTH *MIRROR* OR ANYTHING!

JUST A BRIEF SIDEWAYS SQUINT AT A *REFLECTING POOL!*

IT TOOK SOME TIME...BUT ULTIMATELY, THE CITIZENS OF THE VERY LARGE NATION *DID* COME TO TERMS WITH WHAT THEY HAD BECOME...SORT OF...

NO DOUBT ABOUT IT--MISTAKES OF SOME SORT *WERE* MADE!

BUT I'M SURE IT WILL *NEVER* HAPPEN AGAIN!

SO! ANYTHING GOOD ON *TV* TONIGHT?

THIS MODERN WORLD

by TOM TOMORROW

THEN AND NOW
WITH GOOFUS AND GALLANT

GOOFUS OPPOSED MANY THINGS THE BUSH ADMINISTRATION ACTUALLY **DID**.

TORTURE, WARRANTLESS WIRETAPPING AND A WAR BASED ON **LIES**, FOR STARTERS!

GALLANT OPPOSES MANY THINGS HE IMAGINES THE OBAMA ADMINISTRATION **MIGHT** DO!

THEY'RE SECRETLY PLOTTING TO TURN THE ENTIRE NORTH AMERICAN CONTINENT INTO A **GIANT SOCIALIST COLLECTIVE**!

I READ ABOUT IT ON THE **INTERNET**!

GOOFUS WAS IGNORED, MARGINALIZED, AND LABELED A **KOOK**!

SON, YOUR BUSH-HATRED IS **PROFOUNDLY** UNSERIOUS!

WHY CAN'T YOU BE MORE LIKE **GALLANT**?

GALLANT HAS A NATIONAL TV SHOW AND FRIENDS IN **CONGRESS**!

WAKE **UP** AMERICA-- BEFORE OBAMA ENSLAVES US **ALL** WITH **MANDATORY HEALTH CARE**!

YOU **TELL** 'EM, G!

GOOFUS WAS ARRESTED FOR WEARING THE WRONG **T-SHIRT** TO A BUSH RALLY!

WE DON'T KNOW **WHAT** A TROUBLEMAKER LIKE **YOU** MIGHT DO!

BUT-- BUT--

STOP THE WAR

GALLANT TAKES HIS **ASSAULT RIFLE** TO OBAMA'S TOWN HALL MEETINGS!

THE RIGHT OF THE PEOPLE TO KEEP AND BEAR ARMS IN THE VICINITY OF THE PRESIDENT SHALL NOT BE **INFRINGED**!

GOOFUS WAS REPEATEDLY ACCUSED OF **TREASON**!

IF YOU HATE THE PRESIDENT SO MUCH--WHY DON'T YOU JUST MOVE TO **FRANCE**?

ER--I-- WHAT?

STOP THE

GALLANT LOVES THIS COUNTRY SO MUCH HE WANTS TO **SECEDE**!

THE TREE OF LIBERTY MUST BE REFRESHED FROM TIME TO TIME WITH THE BLOOD OF PATRIOTS AND **TYRANTS**!

WHAT A **GREAT AMERICAN**!

POOR GOOFUS! CAN'T HE GET **ANYTHING** RIGHT?

TOM TOMORROW©2009

THIS MODERN WORLD

by TOM TOMORROW

IN OUR AWESOME POST-RACIAL SOCIETY...

...THE PRESIDENT IS EXPECTED TO HAVE AN OPINION EVERY TIME A BLACK PERSON MISBEHAVES--JUST, YOU KNOW, *BECAUSE!*

SIR--WHAT DO YOU THINK ABOUT THE TEENAGERS WHO GLOWERED MENACINGLY AT ME ON THE *METRO* THIS MORNING?

ER, I-- WHAT?

...TENS OF THOUSANDS* OF ANGRY WHITE CONSERVATIVES GATHER TO TAKE THEIR COUNTRY *BACK*--FROM UNSPECIFIED INTERLOPERS WHOSE RACE IS *ENTIRELY IRRELEVANT!*

WE DON'T CARE IF A PERSON IS BLACK, GREEN OR *PURPLE!*

AS LONG AS THEY'RE NOT BLACK.

OR PRES- IDENT.

BAMA CARE
Coming soon to a clinic near you

THE ANTI- CHRIST

* ELEVENTY-GAZILLION, IF YOU BELIEVE GLENN BECK.

...RIGHT-WING "BIRTHERS" ARE OBSESSED WITH OBAMA'S BIRTH CERTIFICATE--FOR REASONS HAVING *NOTHING WHATSOEVER* TO DO WITH RACE!

WE WOULD HAVE SCRUTINIZED JOHN McCAIN WITH *EQUAL* FERVOR!

THAT'S GREAT! BECAUSE HE REALLY *WAS* BORN OUTSIDE OF THE U.S!

SAY WHAT?

...REPUBLICAN PARENTS VOCIFEROUSLY OBJECT TO A PRESIDENTIAL ADDRESS URGING THEIR KIDS TO *STUDY*... BUT AGAIN: NOTHING TO DO WITH *YOU-KNOW-WHAT*...

HE WANTS TO INDOCTRINATE OUR YOUTH! THE ANSWER IS HIDDEN IN *PLAIN SIGHT!*

Socialist Totalitarian UnAmerican Death Panels You'll be sorry!

AND...GUN-TOTING TEABAGGERS ARE *VERY OFFENDED* WHEN THEIR ENTIRELY REASONABLE STATE- MENTS AND ACTIONS ARE CITED AS EVIDENCE OF *BIGOTRY!*

IT'S GETTING SO A FELLA CAN'T EVEN WEAR A POINTY HOOD AND BURN A CROSS--WITHOUT BEING ACCUSED OF *RACISM!*

WHAT IS THIS COUNTRY *COMING* TO?

TOM TOMORROW©2009

THIS MODERN WORLD

by TOM TOMORROW

LANGUAGE IS A VIRUS

AN OCCASIONAL LOOK AT THE WAYS IN WHICH STUPID IDEAS INFECT POLITICAL DISCOURSE

THIS WEEK: A REAL-LIFE **CASE STUDY!**

1. TOWN HALL/TEA PARTY PROTESTERS CARRY SIGNS PROMINENTLY EQUATING OBAMA WITH HITLER.

REASONED PUBLIC DEBATE **IS** THE FOUNDATION UPON WHICH OUR DEMOCRACY RESTS!

HEIL OBAMA

Fascist

I QUITE CONCUR!

2. DEMOCRATIC POLITICIAN REFERENCES THIS WIDELY-ACKNOWLEDGED FACT.

"AND THEY'RE ATTENDING TOWN HALL RALLIES WITH THESE NAZI SYMBOLS..."

3. DEMOGOGUES WITH MICROPHONES DELIBERATELY MISCONSTRUE POLITICIAN'S REMARK.

YOU SHOULD BE **OUTRAGED!** NANCY **PELOSI** THINKS YOU'RE ALL A BUNCH OF **NAZIS** MARCHING AROUND WITH **SWASTIKAS!**

HERE'S AN OUT-OF-CONTEXT SOUND BITE TO **PROVE** IT!

NAZI SYMBOLS... NAZI SYMBOLS...

4. DELIBERATELY MISCONSTRUED REMARK IS QUICKLY ADDED TO THE GRAND MYTHOLOGY OF RIGHT-WING VICTIMHOOD.

I CAN'T **BELIEVE** AN ELECTED REPRESENTATIVE WOULD SO CALLOUSLY REFER TO AMERICAN CITIZENS WITH WHOM SHE DISAGREES AS **NAZIS!**

HOW CAN WE **POSSIBLY** PURSUE A REASONED PUBLIC DEBATE IN THE FACE OF SUCH **SLANDER?**

5. PROTESTERS **CONTINUE** TO EQUATE OBAMA WITH HITLER.

LOOK! THERE'S A SWASTIKA! RIGHT THERE ON YOUR **SIGN!**

ARE YOU CALLING US **NAZIS?** HEY EVERYBODY--THE PENGUIN THINKS WE'RE **NAZIS!**

HEIL OBAMA

WILL THE NAME-CALLING NEVER **CEASE?**

TOM TOMORROW©2009

THIS MODERN WORLD

by TOM TOMORROW

CLEAR-EYED CONSERVATIVE REALISM

TRANSLATED INTO ENGLISH

WASN'T IT **GREAT** RIGHT AFTER 9/11, WHEN THE COUNTRY WAS SO **UNITED?***

*WASN'T IT GREAT WHEN THE LIBERALS ALL HAD TO SHUT THE HELL UP FOR AWHILE?

NOW IT'S AS IF EVERYONE HAS COMPLETELY FORGOTTEN THAT THE ATTACKS EVER **HAPPENED!***

*LIBERALS NO LONGER KEEP QUIET WHEN I SAY SOMETHING STUPID!

I HATE TO SAY IT--*

*I DON'T HATE TO SAY IT AT ALL.

--BUT IT MIGHT TAKE AN EVEN **WORSE** TERRORIST ATTACK TO SHAKE PEOPLE OUT OF THEIR **COMPLACENCY!***

*LOSING AN AMERICAN CITY IS A SMALL PRICE TO PAY IF IT SHUTS THE LIBERALS UP AGAIN.

WELL--IT'S TOO BAD **EVERYONE** ISN'T AS CLEAR-EYED AND REALISTIC AS **WE** ARE!*

I'LL SECOND **THAT!** **

*WE ARE INSANE SOCIOPATHS! PLEASE, FOR THE LOVE OF GOD, DO NOT PAY ANY ATTENTION TO ANYTHING WE SAY!

** I'LL SECOND **THAT!**

TOM TOMORROW©2009

THIS MODERN WORLD

by TOM TOMORROW

THE IDEA OF OBAMA

THERE IS THE **ACTUAL** OBAMA. WE WILL **END** INDEFINITE DETENTION AND **CLOSE** GUANTANAMO!

AFTER WE ENACT **PRE-EMPTIVE** DETENTION AND EXPAND **BAGRAM**!

AND WE WILL BEGIN TO WITH-DRAW FROM AFGHANISTAN...

...AFTER WE SEND MORE TROOPS.

AND THEN THERE IS THE **IDEA** OF OBAMA.

NEVER MIND **HIM**! I'M EVERY-THING YOU **WANT** ME TO BE!

?

SOMETIMES IT'S EASY TO CONFUSE THE TWO.

I WILL ENACT **TRUE** UNIVERSAL HEALTH CARE, END **BOTH** WARS, AND ERADICATE EVERY **VESTIGE** OF THE BUSH ADMINISTRATION'S WAR ON CIVIL LIBERTIES--AND THAT'S JUST FOR **STARTERS**!

IT'S UNCANNY! HE'S EXACTLY AS I **IMAGINED** HIM!

LATE LAST WEEK, THE IDEA OF OBAMA EVEN WON THE **NOBEL PEACE PRIZE**!

ON BEHALF OF A GRATEFUL WORLD, WE BESTOW THIS HONOR UPON YOU IN RECOGNITION OF ALL THE THINGS WE IMAGINE THAT YOU MIGHT DO.

AND FOR NOT BEING GEORGE W. BUSH.

I AM DEEPLY HUMBLED.

AND THEN THERE IS THE **OTHER** IDEA OF OBAMA.

HEH HEH HEH! WITH THE HELP OF **ACORN** AND MY **FAKE BIRTH CERTIFICATE**, I WILL SOON TRANSFORM THIS COUNTRY INTO A TOTALITARIAN SOCIALIST **NIGHTMARE**!

IT'S UNCANNY! HE'S EXACTLY AS I **IMAGINED** HIM!

TOM TOMORROW©2009

THIS MODERN WORLD
by TOM TOMORROW

Panel 1: THEY DENIED REALITY.

GLOBAL WARMING IS A LIBERAL *HOAX!*

SARAH PALIN IS *TOTALLY* QUALIFIED TO BE PRESIDENT!

Panel 2: THEY DISTORTED REALITY.

THE DEMOCRAT PARTY HAS ONLY ONE GOAL-- TO *DESTROY AMERICA!*

WE'RE ON THE ROAD TO A *SOCIALIST TAKEOVER!*

Panel 3: THEY REWROTE REALITY.

GEORGE W. BUSH WASN'T A *REAL* CONSERVATIVE!

BARACK OBAMA ISN'T A *REAL* AMERICAN CITIZEN!

Panel 4: IN WAYS BIG AND SMALL, CONSERVATIVES UNDERMINED THE VERY CONCEPT OF REALITY--UNTIL ONE DAY REALITY COULD NO LONGER STAND THE STRAIN.

KER-RAAASSSSSH!

URK.

UH OH.

Panel 5: HUMANS WERE SUDDENLY ADRIFT IN A UNIVERSE DEVOID OF HISTORY AND SCIENCE... A PLACE WHERE RATIONALITY HELD NO SWAY.

THE FOUNDING FATHERS *NEVER* INTENDED TO SEPARATE CHURCH AND STATE!

AND THEY WERE 17 FEET TALL AND HAD ADAMANTIUM BONES!

Panel 6: NEEDLESS TO SAY, MANY PEOPLE FOUND IT ALL EXTREMELY DISTURBING.

WITHOUT THE MOST FUNDAMENTAL CONSENSUS REALITY--HOW CAN SOCIETY *FUNCTION?*

SOME DAYS YOU JUST CAN'T HOLD ONTO YOUR *HEAD!*

DANGER WILL ROBINSON!

Panel 7: BUT MOST CONSERVATIVES FELT PERFECTLY AT HOME.

WOO HOO! SARAH PALIN *IS* QUALIFIED TO BE PRESIDENT!

AND MONKEYS *CAN* FLY OUT OF BODILY ORIFICES!

REALITY ALWAYS *WAS* OVERRATED, IF YOU ASK *ME!*

THIS MODERN WORLD

by TOM TOMORROW

Panel 1: RIGHT-WING ACTIVISTS RECENTLY CAUGHT SOME REGRETTABLY ACCOMODATING--AND GULLIBLE--ACORN EMPLOYEES ON *VIDEO*...

HELLO! I AM A *PIMP*, YO! AND THIS IS MY *HO*, YO!

YO HO HO!

ER--OKAY THEN!

Panel 2: ...THEREBY EXPOSING THE *GREATEST MENACE* FACING OUR NATION TODAY!

TODAY COMMUNITIES • TOMORROW THE WORLD

A. C. O. R. N.*

*AMERICA-HATING COMMUNOFASCISTS ORGANIZED FOR REVOLUTION NOW!

Panel 3: FROM THEIR CLANDESTINE HEAD-QUARTERS INSIDE A HOLLOWED-OUT VOLCANO, THE ACORNISTAS PURSUE THEIR *NEFARIOUS AGENDA*!

WE'RE LUCKY WE FINISHED CONSTRUCTION BEFORE THE AMERICANS CUT OFF OUR *FUNDING*!

THESE CLANDESTINE VOLCANO HEADQUARTERS DON'T COME *CHEAP*!

Panel 4: IT IS THERE THAT ACORN'S SECRET LEADER, *GEORGE SOROS*, OVERSEES THEIR PLANS FOR *WORLD DOMINATION*!

BWAH HA HA! WITH OUR BRAINWASHED *PUPPET* INSTALLED IN THE WHITE HOUSE--*NOTHING* CAN STOP US NOW!

BUT WAIT-- WHAT'S *THIS*?

Panel 5: IT'S THE ONE PERSON WHO *CAN* STOP ACORN--THE COOL, COMPOSED, NEARLY *EMOTIONLESS* MAN KNOWN AS...*AGENT BECK*!

YOU'RE *FINISHED*, SOROS! I KNOW ALL *ABOUT* YOUR PLANS TO TEAM UP WITH THE *SEIU* AND THE *NEA* TO *DESTROY AMERICA AS WE KNOW IT*!

PLEASE DISPOSE OF THIS TEDIOUS MAN.

Panel 6: BUT...IF AGENT BECK *CAN'T* DEFEAT THE FORCES OF ACORN--IS AMERICA *DOOMED*?

HA HA HA! *NO ONE* CAN DEFEAT MY MIGHTY ARMY OF REGIONAL COMMUNITY ORGANIZERS WITH A FOCUS ON LOW-INCOME HOUSING ADVOCACY AND VOTER REGISTRATION!

EVERYTHING IS UNFOLDING EXACTLY AS WOODROW WILSON* *PLANNED*!

YOU WON'T GET AWAY WITH THIS, YOU--YOU PROGRESSIVE *FIEND*!

*HISTORY'S GREATEST MONSTER, ACCORDING TO BECK.

THIS MODERN WORLD

by TOM TOMORROW

Panel 1: ARE YOU OKAY? YOU LOOK *BEAT!*

OH, I'VE JUST BEEN FEELING A LITTLE RUN DOWN LATELY...SPARKY, WHAT'S HAPPENED TO CONSERVATIVES SINCE OBAMA WON? DID THEY ALL LOSE THEIR MINDS *SIMULTANEOUSLY?*

Panel 2: I MEAN, TEA PARTIES, DEATH PANELS, BIRTH CERTIFICATES...GLENN BECK'S WEIRD CONSPIRACY THEORIES ABOUT EARLY TWENTIETH CENTURY PROGRESSIVES AND WOODROW WILSON AND...AND...

WELL, BASICALLY EVERYTHING GLENN BECK *SAYS...*

YAWN...

Panel 3: AND ALL THESE GUYS BRANDISHING GUNS OUTSIDE OF OBAMA EVENTS-- SERIOUSLY, WHAT'S *UP* WITH THAT? AND WHAT ABOUT THE NEWSMAX COLUMNIST WHO SUGGESTED THAT THE "OBAMA PROBLEM" COULD BE SOLVED WITH A *MILITARY COUP?*

YAWWWNNN...EXCUSE ME...I REALLY NEED TO GET SOME REST...

Panel 4: *AND*--YAWN--WHAT ABOUT THE RIGHT'S EUPHORIA OVER OBAMA'S FAILED OLYMPIC BID? AND THEIR NEWFOUND CONTEMPT FOR *CHICAGO*--ALONG WITH THE NORTHEAST, THE WEST COAST, PRETTY MUCH ANY LARGE METROPOLITAN AREA OR COLLEGE TOWN...MOST OF THE *COUNTRY*, REALLY...

Panel 5: NOT TO MENTION THE PARANOIA OVER THE *CENSUS*...THE MELTDOWN OVER A PRESIDENTIAL SPEECH TO *SCHOOLCHILDREN*...THE ENDLESS OBSESSION WITH *ACORN*...AND...UM...

IF YOU'LL EXCUSE ME I THINK I'M JUST GOING TO TAKE A LITTLE...

NAP...

?

THUNK!

Panel 6: WHAT HAPPENED TO *HIM?*

IT'S ANOTHER CASE OF *CRAZY FATIGUE.*

SOMETIMES THE SHEER OVERWHELMING MAGNITUDE OF RIGHT WING LUNACY IS MORE THAN THE HUMAN MIND CAN BEAR.

--AND... ANOTHER THING...

I'LL CALL 9-1-1.

ZZZZZZ

Tom Tomorrow©2009

THIS MODERN WORLD

by TOM TOMORROW

WELL, WE'RE OFF TO THIS YEAR'S *HALLOWEEN PARTY!*

ISN'T A SARAH PALIN COSTUME KIND OF *PASSÉ* AT THIS POINT?

CENSUS

I'M NOT JUST SARAH PALIN--I'M THE TERRIFYING PROSPECT OF FUTURE *PRESIDENT* SARAH PALIN, ELECTED AS A RESULT OF MASS VOTER INSANITY AND/OR RIGGED VOTING MACHINES!

CENSUS

I MAKE GEORGE W. BUSH LOOK LIKE A *NUCLEAR PHYSICIST!* I CAN'T EVEN NAME A *NEWSPAPER* I READ REGULARLY--AND NOW THE FATE OF THE ENTIRE WORLD IS IN *MY HANDS!*

BWAH HA HA HA HA!

CENSUS

SERIOUSLY, THE MERE THOUGHT OF IT KEEPS ME AWAKE AT NIGHT.

YEAH, I GET IT. AND YOUR LITTLE *SIDE-KICK* THERE?

WHY THAT'S VICE PRESIDENT *MICHELE BACHMANN,* OF COURSE!

I DON'T KNOW WHY *I* ALWAYS GET DRAGGED INTO THESE THINGS.

CENSUS

I WANTED TO DRESS UP AS *EDDIE VEDDER!*

TOM TOMORROW©2009

71

WELCOME TO GLOX NEWS! OUR TOP STORY THIS MICRO-INSTANT: THE PARTY CURRENTLY IN POWER *CONTINUES* ITS MISGUIDED AT-TEMPT TO REFORM THE SYSTEM BY WHICH WE OF THE NORTHERN LAND MASS ATTEND TO INJURIES AND ILLNESS!

THE PARTY WHICH *SHOULD* BE IN POWER CONTINUES TO *OPPOSE* SUCH EFFORTS!

AND RIGHTLY SO! IF A SENTIENT HAS NOT ACCUMULATED ENOUGH SHINY STONES TO PAY FOR BIO-LOGICAL UPKEEP AND REPAIRS-- WHY *SHOULDN'T* HE BE ABAN-DONED ON THE NORTHERNMOST PLAINS TO BE DISMEMEBERED AND EVENTUALLY CONSUMED BY THE BEASTS WHICH ROAM THERE?

SOMETIMES THE OLD WAYS *ARE* BEST!

SHOCKINGLY, THE CURRENT RULING PARTY INTENDS TO IMPLEMENT THEIR REFORM--UNDER WHICH *SOMEWHAT FEWER* SENTIENTS WOULD BE ABANDONED ON THE NORTHERNMOST PLAINS--WITH A SIMPLE *MAJORITY VOTE*, RATHER THAN THE *QUAD-RUPLE* MAJORITY WHICH UNWRITTEN TRADITION *DEMANDS!*

IN OTHER WORDS, THEY'RE GOING TO *RAM IT DOWN OUR FEEDING TUBES!*

YES--AND SUCH BLATANT DISRE-SPECT FOR THE VALUES AND TRA-DITIONS OF OUR LAND MASS CAN *ONLY* LEAD TO ECONOMIC CHAOS AND SOCIETAL UPHEAVAL! BUT THERE ARE *THREE SUPPORT-TENTACLES OF STRENGTH*, UPON WHICH *TRUE* SENTIENTS KNOW THEY CAN RELY--

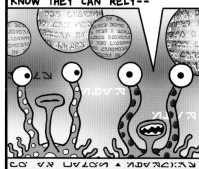

--AN UNWAVERING FAITH IN THE ONE TRUE GROUPING OF *DEITIES*-- A LARGE STOCKPILE OF PERSONAL *FUSION WEAPONS*--

--AND THE INVESTMENT-GRADE *SHINY STONES* OFFERED BY THE MER-CHANT-CASTE SPONSORS OF *THIS INFOCAST!*

COMING UP NEXT: DOES OUR CUR-RENT SUPREME LEADER ACTUALLY *BELIEVE* IN THE DOMINANT IDEOLOGY OF OUR LAND MASS--OR IS HE SECRETLY AN ADHERENT OF AN ENTIRELY *DIFFERENT* IDEOLOGY?

AND--*WHY* WON'T HE UNVEIL THE TABLETS OF CERTIFICATION TO VERIFY THE SPATIAL COORDINATES OF HIS *CONCEPTION*?

FIRST THESE MESSAGES FROM THE MERCHANT CASTE.

TOM TOMORROW © 2010

THIS MODERN WORLD

by TOM TOMORROW

THIS WEEK: ANOTHER MYSTERY FROM THE CASEFILES OF *CONSERVATIVE JONES, BOY DETECTIVE!*

BACK IN THE TREEHOUSE, I SEE.

VERY OBSERVANT OF YOU, MOONBAT! PERHAPS WE'LL MAKE A BOY DETECTIVE OUT OF YOU *YET!* THOUGH I DOUBT IT.

(FEATURING THE EVER-HAPLESS *MOONBAT McWACKY!*)

NOW PAY ATTENTION! I'M WORKING ON THE MYSTERY OF *HEALTH CARE REFORM*--AND THE GAME'S *AFOOT!*

OH, THIS SHOULD BE GOOD.

YOU SEE, WE HAVE THE BEST HEALTH CARE SYSTEM IN THE *WORLD!* HOW CAN YOU IMPROVE UPON *PERFECTION?* QUITE CLEARLY, MY DEAR MOONBAT, YOU *CANNOT!* SO WHY DO DEMOCRATS PERSIST IN *TRYING?*

ER--WELL--LEAVING ASIDE THE QUESTION OF WHETHER THE WATERED-DOWN, INSURER-FRIENDLY BILL WE'RE LIKELY TO GET EVEN *QUALIFIES* AS "REFORM"--

--COULD IT BE BECAUSE MILLIONS OF AMERICANS HAVE NO HEALTH INSURANCE? BECAUSE INSURANCE COMPANIES ROUTINELY DENY CARE AND DROP COVERAGE? BECAUSE OUR PATCHWORK SYSTEM OF FOR-PROFIT, EMPLOYER-BASED HEALTH INSURANCE FUNDAMENTALLY MAKES NO SENSE *WHATSOEVER?*

OH, MOONBAT! DO DELIGHTFUL CARTOON ANIMALS FROLIC THROUGH THE FORESTS OF THE FANTASY WORLD IN WHICH YOU SPEND YOUR TIME?

NO, THE ANSWER IS MUCH SIMPLER! LIBERALS WANT TO "REFORM" THE HEALTH CARE SYSTEM...BECAUSE THEY *HATE THE FREE MARKET!*

THAT SEEMS TO BE THE SOLUTION TO A *LOT* OF YOUR CASES.

CEASE YOUR *PRATTLE*, MOONBAT! I'M ON TO MY *NEXT* CASE-- THE MYSTERY OF HOW THIS COUNTRY WAS TAKEN AWAY FROM *REAL* AMERICANS--SUCH AS *MYSELF!*

OH--I KNOW THIS ONE! THERE WAS AN *ELECTION*--

DON'T YOU HAVE A FLAG TO BURN OR SOMETHING?

NEXT: YOU'RE EITHER PART OF THE SOLUTION--OR YOU'RE A TOOL OF *ACORN!*

TOM TOMORROW©2009

THIS MODERN WORLD

by TOM TOMORROW

JOE & HARRY

STARRING THE MOST IMPORTANT POLITICIAN IN ALL OF HUMAN HISTORY, **JOE LIEBERMAN**

YA KNOW, JOE, I'VE OFTEN TOLD PEOPLE THAT YOU'RE "WITH DEMOCRATS ON EVERYTHING BUT THE WAR."

UH HUH.

SO I'M PROPOSING A **PUBLIC OPTION**--

I'M NOT WITH YOU ON THAT.

DON'T WORRY! IT'S A WATERED-DOWN VERSION WITH AN **"OPT-OUT"** PROVISION!

STILL NOT WITH YOU.

HUH.

DID I MENTION THAT YOUR INSURANCE INDUSTRY BACKERS WILL LIKELY BE THE ONES **ADMINISTERING** A PUBLIC OPTION?

NOT GOOD ENOUGH.

WELL--WHAT ABOUT A PUBLIC OPTION WITH A "CROSSED OUR FINGERS BEHIND OUR BACKS SO IT DOESN'T REALLY **COUNT**" CLAUSE?

NOPE.

A PUBLIC OPTION ONLY AVAILABLE ON THE SECOND TUESDAY IN MARCH DURING ALTERNATE **LEAP YEARS**?

NUH-UH.

A PUBLIC OPTION WHICH EXCLUDES PARTICIPATION BY ANY **CARBON-BASED LIFE FORM**?

SORRY.

OKAY, OKAY--A PUBLIC OPTION REQUIRING DEMOCRATS TO APOLOGIZE **PROFUSELY** FOR NOT SUPPORTING JOE LIEBERMAN IN 2006.

NOW YOU'RE TALKING.

BUT SOON THEREAFTER...

WAIT--YOU'RE **STILL** GOING TO FILIBUSTER?

REVENGE IS A DISH BEST SERVED OVER AND OVER AND OVER AGAIN.

AS WE IN THE CONNECTICUT-FOR-LIEBERMAN PARTY LIKE TO SAY.

TOM TOMORROW©2009

THIS MODERN WORLD

by TOM TOMORROW

THE STUPIDITY CRISIS

IN AN AMAZING BREAKTHROUGH, SCIENTISTS DISCOVER A WAY TO EXTRACT ENERGY FROM A SEEMINGLY LIMITLESS RESOURCE--**HUMAN STUPIDITY!**

EUREKA! IT'S **WORKING!** SOON WE'LL BE ABLE TO **END** OUR SOCIETY'S DEPENDENCE ON FOSSIL FUELS!

BUT--WHY WOULD WE WANT TO DO **THAT**?

SOON AVERAGE CITIZENS ACROSS THE NATION ARE PROVIDING THE POWER OF **STUPIDITY!**

I THINK SARAH PALIN WOULD MAKE A **TERRIFIC** PRESIDENT!

ACORN IS THE GREATEST THREAT TO DEMOCRACY **EVER**!

WE'RE ONE STEP AWAY FROM A MARXIST **DICTATORSHIP!**

BLAH BLAH **BLAH!**

BUT THEN--AN UNEXPECTED **PROBLEM** DEVELOPS...

UM...WHY WERE WE SO OBSESSED WITH ACORN, EXACTLY?

I--I CAN'T **REMEMBER**...

OH MY GOD--WE'VE DRAINED THEM OF **ALL STUPIDITY!** THE POWER GRID WILL **COLLAPSE!**

THE GOVERNMENT INITIATES A CRASH PROGRAM TO **REPLENISH** THE NATION'S STUPIDITY RESERVES.

--AND EVERY CHANNEL ON TV WILL BROADCAST **GLENN BECK** RERUNS TWENTY-FOUR HOURS A DAY!

IF THAT DOESN'T DO IT--**NOTHING** WILL!

THE CRISIS IS AVERTED--BUT **THEN**--

I'VE GOT AN IDEA! LET'S DITCH THE HELMETS--AND **RESTORE** OUR DEPENDENCE ON **FOSSIL FUELS!**

THAT WAY, WE'LL NEVER HAVE TO RISK RUNNING OUT OF STUPIDITY **AGAIN!**

IT IS TRULY OUR NATION'S MOST PRECIOUS RESOURCE.

THIS MODERN WORLD

by TOM TOMORROW

Panel 1:

OBAMA'S DECISION TO ESCALATE IN AFGHANISTAN WAS NOT EXACTLY UNEXPECTED.

BUT--BUT--IN OUR MANY IMAGINARY CONVERSATIONS, HE NEVER EVEN **MENTIONED** THE POSSIBILITY!

NOR IN **OURS!**

UH--HE TALKS TO YOU, TOO?

WHAT?

Panel 2:

BUT NEITHER WAS IT THE OUTCOME OF SOME LONG-SETTLED DEBATE.

HE **SAID** HE WOULD DO THIS--AND YOU HAD YOUR CHANCE TO OBJECT, IN **NOVEMBER** OF **2008!**

YOU COULD HAVE VOTED FOR THE **OTHER** CANDIDATE.

WHO **ALSO** PLANNED TO ESCALATE.

BUT YOU DID NOT.

NOW PLEASE BE QUIET UNTIL 2012.

Panel 3:

CANDIDATE OBAMA MADE HIS INTENTIONS FAIRLY CLEAR.

IF ELECTED I WILL SEND AT LEAST **TWO** MORE BRIGADES INTO AFGHANISTAN, BECAUSE THAT IS A **GOOD** WAR, UNLIKE IRAQ, WHICH I ALONE AMONG MY RIVALS HAD THE FORESIGHT AND WISDOM TO **OPPOSE!**

GOT IT?

Panel 4:

BUT A LOT OF PEOPLE WERE PAYING MORE ATTENTION TO THE **IDEA** OF OBAMA BACK THEN.

NEVER MIND WHAT HE **SAYS!** SECRETLY HE AGREES WITH YOU--ABOUT **EVERYTHING!**

HA! I **KNEW** IT!

Panel 5:

THESE DAYS, THE DISCONNECT BETWEEN THE MAN AND THE **IDEA** OF THE MAN IS PRETTY HARD TO IGNORE--

OKAY--**I'LL** GIVE THE SPEECH COMMITTING THIS NATION TO SEVERAL MORE YEARS OF BLOODSHED IN **AFGHANISTAN**--

Panel 6:

--AND ABOUT TO GET **MORE** SO.

--AND **YOU** GO OVER TO OSLO AND PICK UP OUR NOBEL PEACE PRIZE.

"OUR" PEACE PRIZE?

ALL RIGHT, ALL RIGHT--**YOUR** PEACE PRIZE.

YOU'RE NOTHING WITHOUT **ME**, YOU KNOW!

BACK ATCHA, CHIEF.

TOM TOMORROW©2009

THIS MODERN WORLD

by TOM TOMORROW

Panel 1:

IT'S JUST NOT THAT COMPLICATED: EVERYONE SHOULD HAVE HEALTH INSURANCE THAT CAN'T BE TAKEN AWAY.

BECAUSE WE ARE MORTAL BEINGS, SUSCEPTIBLE TO ACCIDENTS, ILLNESS, AND THE RAVAGES OF TIME.

OR AS THE INSURANCE INDUSTRY CALLS THEM, "PRE-EXISTING CONDITIONS."

Panel 2:

NONETHELESS, REPUBLICANS ARE DOING EVERYTHING POSSIBLE TO SLOW-WALK HEALTH CARE REFORM TO OBLIVION.

NONSENSE! WE JUST WANT TO CAREFULLY CONSIDER EVERY POSSIBLE OPTION FOR A VERY, VERY, *VERY* LONG TIME!

A PROCESS WHICH IS DEFINITELY NOT TO BE CONFUSED WITH "DITHERING."

Panel 3:

ONE ACTUAL REPUBLICAN ARGUMENT AGAINST REFORM: IT WILL BE *TOO POPULAR!*

THE PUBLIC WILL BE SO GRATEFUL TO DEMOCRATS FOR SOLVING THIS FUNDAMENTAL DILEMMA OF AMERICAN LIFE, REPUBLICANS WILL NEVER BE ABLE TO REGAIN POWER *AGAIN!*

IT'S DIABOLICAL, I TELL YOU -- *DIABOLICAL!*

Panel 4:

MEANWHILE, HOUSE DEMOCRATS JUST PASSED A HEALTH CARE REFORM BILL WHICH WOULD SEVERELY *RESTRICT* REPRODUCTIVE HEALTH OPTIONS FOR MILLIONS OF WOMEN.

IN ORDER TO GET THE VOTES THEY NEEDED, THEY JUST HAD TO DO A LITTLE "HORSE TRADING"!

SURE -- WITH THE CONSTITUTIONAL RIGHTS OF HALF THE POPULATION.

Panel 5:

THINK ABOUT IT: NO ONE *CARES* WHETHER YOU WANT YOUR TAX DOLLARS SPENT ON POINTLESS *WARS* --

I OBJECT ON MORAL GROUNDS!

SO GO WHINE ABOUT IT ON YOUR *BLOG!*

-- BUT *ABORTION* IS ANOTHER STORY ENTIRELY.

I OBJECT ON MORAL GROUNDS!

AND WE WILL BEND OVER *BACKWARDS* TO APPEASE YOU!

Panel 6:

IN ANY EVENT, REPUBLICANS AND DEMOCRATS *HAVE* FINALLY MANAGED TO ACHIEVE BIPARTISAN CONSENSUS ON AT LEAST *ONE* ISSUE -- THE SECOND-CLASS STATUS OF *WOMEN* IN OUR SOCIETY...

THE GOVERNMENT SHOULD *NEVER* COME BETWEEN DOCTORS AND THEIR PATIENTS --

-- EXCEPT WHEN *LADY PARTS* ARE INVOLVED!

TALK ABOUT A *PRE-EXISTING CONDITION!*

TOM TOMORROW©2009

THIS MODERN WORLD

by TOM TOMORROW

THE ASSOCIATION OF RIGHT-WING BEDWETTERS P R E S E N T S

5 EXTREMELY COMPELLING REASONS NOT TO HOLD TERROR TRIALS IN NEW YORK CITY

1) SOME LIBERAL JUDGE MIGHT LET THE TERRORISTS OFF ON A *TECHNICALITY*.

THE AMERICAN JUDICIAL SYSTEM CAN'T BE *TRUSTED*!

THE FOUNDING FATHERS *SHOULD* HAVE INCLUDED A "NO-TRIAL-NECESSARY-IF-YOU-*KNOW*-THEY'RE-GUILTY" CLAUSE!

2) THE REST OF THE WORLD MIGHT LEARN TOO MUCH ABOUT THE AMERICAN TORTURE PROGRAM.

ANY MORE ATTENTION TO THAT BUSINESS ABOUT SLICING DETAINEES' GENITALS WITH *SCALPELS* ISN'T GOING TO WIN US ANY FRIENDS.*

THE REST OF THE WORLD IS *SO* JUDGMENTAL!

*GOOGLE IT.

3) TERRORISTS COULD USE THE TRIAL TO SPREAD THEIR HATEFUL IDEOLOGY.

AND THEN THE NEXT THING YOU KNOW OUR KIDS WILL ALL BE RUNNING OFF TO JOIN THE *JIHAD*! IS *THAT* WHAT YOU WANT?

OUR LEGAL SYSTEM IS FOR DEFENDANTS WITH *PLEASANT* THINGS TO DISCUSS!

4) SINCE THE TRIAL COULD PUT NEW YORK CITY AT RISK, IT SHOULD BE HELD SOMEWHERE ELSE SO OTHER PEOPLE ARE PUT AT RISK INSTEAD.

THESE TERRORISTS--THEY'RE *SUPERVILLAINS*! THEY'RE LIKE *LEX LUTHOR* OR SOMETHING!

CAN'T WE JUST HOLD A *TRIBUNAL*--IN THE *NEGATIVE ZONE*?

5) WE'RE VERY, VERY AFRAID.

IT HAS BEEN THE DEFINING PRINCIPLE OF OUR LIVES FOR MORE THAN EIGHT YEARS.

WE'RE DAMN SURE NOT GIVING IT UP *NOW*.

OOPS! I THINK I JUST WET MYSELF.

WHO CAN *BLAME* YOU?

TOM TOMORROW©2009

THIS MODERN WORLD

by TOM TOMORROW

2009 THE YEAR IN CRAZY

PART THE FIRST

JAN. 11: JOE THE PLUMBER OPINES--

"I DON'T THINK JOURNALISTS SHOULD BE ALLOWED ANYWHERE NEAR WAR...I THINK MEDIA SHOULD BE ABOLISHED FROM, YOU KNOW, *REPORTING!*"

JAN. 20: CHIEF JUSTICE FLUBS OATH OF OFFICE; WINGNUTS FLIP OUT.

OBAMA DIDN'T SAY THE MAGIC WORDS! HE'S NOT *REALLY* PRESIDENT!

JAN. 22: OBAMA TAKES SECOND OATH OF OFFICE-- BUT WITHOUT A BIBLE. WINGNUTS FLIP OUT.

THEY DIDN'T USE THE MAGIC BOOK! HE'S *STILL* NOT REALLY PRESIDENT!

FEB. 24: IN HIGH-PROFILE SPEECH BOBBY JINDAL MOCKS "SOMETHING CALLED VOLCANO MONITORING."

A MONTH LATER, VOLCANO ERUPTION IN ALASKA SENDS ASH CLOUDS 50,000 FEET INTO THE AIR.

MONTH OF MARCH: RIGHT-WING BLOGGERS START THREATENING TO "GO GALT."

WE'LL TAKE OUR PRODUCTIVITY AND *GO HOME!*

AMERICANS SOMEHOW RESIST URGE TO PANIC.

ALSO: WINGNUTS NOTICE THAT PRESIDENTS USE TELEPROMPTERS; APPARENTLY THIS IS NEWS TO THEM.

HA HA! HIM NOT SO SMART! HIM READ WORDS OFF FUNNY SCREEN!

APRIL 9: NOT-AT-ALL CRAZY GLENN BECK PRETENDS TO POUR GAS ON A GUY AND LIGHT HIM ON FIRE.

NOT MUCH WE CAN ADD TO THAT.

APRIL 15: WINGERS CLAIM ONE MILLION ATTENDEES AT TEA PARTY PROTEST.

IT WAS ONE OF THE BIGGEST RALLIES IN HUMAN *HISTORY!*

THEY ARE ONLY OFF BY 950,000 OR SO.

APR. 16: GOV. PERRY SUGGESTS TEXAS COULD SECEDE FROM UNION.

WE LOVE AMERICA SO MUCH, WE'RE READY TO *DESTROY* IT!

APRIL 22: CORNERED BY GUEST, SEAN HANNITY RELUCTANTLY AGREES TO BE WATERBOARDED FOR CHARITY.

SURE...NO BIG DEAL... HEH HEH...

NEVER FOLLOWS THROUGH.

APRIL 28: MICHELE BACHMANN NOTES THAT LAST SWINE FLU OUTBREAK ALSO BEGAN UNDER DEMOCRATIC PRESIDENT, CALLS IT "INTERESTING COINCIDENCE."

ACTUALLY LAST OUTBREAK BEGAN UNDER GERALD FORD--AS IF IT REMOTELY *MATTERS...*

MAY 15: BILL O'REILLY, WHO ROUTINELY SENDS CAMERA CREWS OUT TO HARASS PEOPLE, SAYS:

"AMERICANS SHOULD BE ABLE TO GO OUT...WITHOUT BEING HARASSED BY PEOPLE WITH CAMERAS!"

JUNE 16: "FAMILY VALUES" REPUBLICAN JOHN ENSIGN CAUGHT IN SEX SCANDAL.

OOPS!

JUNE 24: "FAMILY VALUES" REPUBLICAN MARK SANFORD CAUGHT IN SEX SCANDAL.

MY BAD!

JUNE 17: HOUSE REPUBLICANS COMPARE SELVES TO IRANIAN DISSIDENTS.

WE ARE JUST LIKE THEM, BUT WITH MORE SEX SCANDALS.

JUNE 29: 200+ PEOPLE SHOW UP FOR "TAKE YOUR GUN TO CHURCH DAY" IN KENTUCKY.

PRAISE THE LORD AND PASS THE AMMUNITION!

NEXT WEEK: MORE CRAZY!

TOM TOMORROW©2009

THIS MODERN WORLD

by TOM TOMORROW

2009 THE YEAR IN CRAZY

PART THE SECOND

JULY 1: JOE THE PLUMBER ANNOUNCES THAT HE HAS NO PLANS TO RUN FOR OFFICE.

"I TALKED TO GOD ABOUT THAT AND HE WAS LIKE, 'NO'."

NON-BELIEVERS ARE GIVEN MOMENTARY PAUSE.

JULY 3: SARAH PALIN ABRUPTLY RESIGNS GOVERNORSHIP. INVENTIVE RATIONALIZATIONS ENSUE.

REAL LEADERS DON'T WASTE TIME *LEADING!*

THEY PURSUE BOOK DEALS AND SPEAKING FEES!

MONTH OF AUGUST: TEABAGGERS ATTEND TOWN HALL MEETINGS; SHOUT ABOUT SOCIALISM, BIRTH CERTIFICATES, AND THE GOVERNMENT FLU VACCINE CONSPIRACY.

ALSO, *ACORN* HAS BEEN STEALING MY *UNDERPANTS!*

MONTH OF AUGUST, CONT'D: TEABAGGERS ALSO KEEP SHOWING UP AT OBAMA EVENTS WITH *GUNS.*

IT'S A LEGITIMATE FORM OF PROTEST!

AND I'LL PLUG ANY VARMINT WHO SEZ *OTHERWISE!*

AUG. 7: EX-GOVERNOR PALIN WARNS OF GOVERNMENT "DEATH PANELS."

I GOT TWO WORDS FOR YA: *SOYLENT GREEN!*

AUG. 19: PROFESSING DOUBT ABOUT THE PRESIDENT'S CITIZENSHIP, TOM DELAY SAYS HE WOULD LIKE TO SEE OBAMA'S "GIFT CERTIFICATE."

I BET IT'S FROM A *KENYAN* DEPARTMENT STORE!

SEPT. 7: RIGHT WING COLLECTIVELY FREAKS OUT OVER PRESIDENTIAL SPEECH TO SCHOOLCHILDREN.

YOU KNOW WHO *ELSE* LIKED TO GIVE SPEECHES?

HITLER!!

SEPT. 12: LIBERALS UNFAIRLY PORTRAY "9-12" PROTESTORS AS RACISTS BY SHOWING PICTURES OF THE SIGNS THEY HELD.

SEPT. 30: NEWSMAX COLUMNIST SUGGESTS THE "OBAMA PROBLEM" COULD BE SOLVED WITH A *MILITARY COUP.*

HEY--I'M JUST *SAYIN'!*

OCT. 2: CONSERVATIVES *CHEER* WHEN COUNTRY LOSES OLYMPIC BID.

WE LOVE AMERICA--WE JUST HATE *CHICAGO!*

ALONG WITH THE EAST COAST, THE WEST COAST, BIG CITIES, BLUE STATES, COLLEGE TOWNS--

OCT. 27: JOE LIEBERMAN THREATENS TO FILIBUSTER ANY HEALTH CARE BILL WITH A PUBLIC OPTION.

WHAT CAN I SAY? I'M JUST AN ASSHOLE.

EARLY NOV.: TOWN HALL TEABAGGERS HECKLE WOMAN WHOSE DAUGHTER-IN-LAW AND UNBORN GRANDCHILD DIED DUE TO LACK OF HEALTH INSURANCE.

WHAT *LOSERS!* SUCH MISFORTUNE COULD *NEVER* BEFALL ME!

NOV. 23: NOT-AT-ALL-CRAZY GLENN BECK ANNOUNCES "100 YEAR PLAN" TO SAVE AMERICA FROM VAST SOCIALIST CONSPIRACY ONLY HE CAN PERCEIVE.

THE VOICES IN MY HEAD EXPLAINED IT *ALL* TO ME!

NOV. 24: DANA PERINO TELLS SEAN HANNITY--

"--WE DID NOT HAVE A TERRORIST ATTACK ON OUR COUNTRY DURING PRESIDENT BUSH'S TERM!"

SERIOUSLY, SHE SAID THAT.

DECEMBER: ANNUAL WAR ON FICTIONAL WAR ON CHRISTMAS COMMENCES...

WAIT--WE'RE OUT OF SPACE ALREADY??

WHAT ABOUT ORLY TAITZ? NAZI SYMBOLS? "GOING ROGUE"? THE CENSUS? ETC. ETC. *ETC!*

...SEE YOU NEXT YEAR!

TOM TOMORROW@2009

THIS MODERN WORLD
by TOM TOMORROW

Panel 1:
WELL, 2009 SURE TURNED INTO QUITE THE ROLLER COASTER RIDE.

DIDN'T START OFF SO WELL, WITH THE LARGEST ALTWEEKLY CHAIN AXING ALL CARTOONS.

Panel 2:
DEFINITELY NOT A GOOD MOMENT... BUT NOT LONG AFTER THAT, MY FRIEND ED CALLED UP AND OFFERED ME A SHOT AT DOING HIS NEXT *ALBUM COVER*...

Panel 3:
THAT PROJECT CONSUMED ME FOR *MONTHS*...THE WHOLE FIRST HALF OF THE YEAR IS KIND OF A BLUR, IN RETROSPECT...

Panel 4:
BUT IN THE END, IT WAS A FANTASTIC EXPERIENCE...I OWE THE ENTIRE BAND A DEBT OF GRATITUDE, FOR PUTTING THEIR TRUST IN ME...

BUT IT WASN'T YOUR *ONLY* BIG PROJECT...

Panel 5:
RIGHT--I ALSO PUBLISHED MY FIRST *CHILDREN'S BOOK*, STARRING A CERTAIN CANTANKEROUS--

--BUT LOVABLE--   --PENGUIN.

AND HIS DOG.

Panel 6:
YOU KNOW, THE THING IS...A YEAR AGO TODAY, I WAS JUST GOING ABOUT MY BUSINESS, HAPPILY OBLIVIOUS...WITH NO WAY OF KNOWING THAT THIS ALTERNATELY DEVASTATING AND EXHILARATING YEAR WAS WAITING JUST AROUND THE CORNER...

Panel 7:
AND NOW WE'RE AT THE START OF AN ENTIRELY *NEW* YEAR! NEW OPPORTUNITIES, NEW CHALLENGES...*ANYTHING* COULD HAPPEN! THE ROAD AHEAD COULD LEAD *ANYWHERE*!

Panel 8:

Panel 9:
IT'S REALLY KIND OF *TERRIFYING* IF YOU THINK ABOUT IT TOO MUCH.

HAPPY NEW YEAR, MISTER GLASS-HALF-FULL.

CAN I LOSE THE *HAT* NOW?

TOM TOMORROW©2009

THIS MODERN WORLD

by TOM TOMORROW

IT'S TIME FOR ANOTHER VISIT TO...
PARALLEL EARTH!

IT IS A WORLD MUCH LIKE OURS... BUT SEE IF YOU CAN SPOT THE **SUBTLE DIFFERENCE!***

--AND SO A PERSON **COULD** BLAME THE HAITI DISASTER ON A "PACT WITH THE DEVIL"--BUT TO DO SO WOULD CLEARLY BE AN ACT OF **MONSTROUS** INSENSITIVITY!

I MEAN, IF YOU MUST VIEW THIS EVENT THROUGH THE LENS OF THE SUPERNATURAL--YOU COULD JUST AS EASILY LOOK AT THE SHEER MAGNITUDE OF PAIN, SUFFERING, AND LOSS, AND CONCLUDE THAT **GOD** IS EITHER UNIMAGINABLY CRUEL--OR DOES NOT EXIST.

BUT HOW IS THAT **HELPFUL**?

AND WHAT KIND OF PERSON WOULD EVEN **SUGGEST** THAT THE VICTIMS OF SUCH DEVASTATION WERE RESPONSIBLE FOR THEIR OWN MISFORTUNE, DUE TO SOME MYTHICAL ANCESTRAL ALLIANCE WITH A SUPERNATURAL BEING?

IT WOULD BE AS ODIOUS AND IRRATIONAL AS BLAMING THE 9/11 ATTACKS ON **FEMINISTS** AND **GAYS!** OR BLAMING HURRICANE KATRINA ON THE LEGALITY OF **ABORTION!** OR SUGGESTING THAT DISNEY WORLD'S "GAY DAYS" WOULD LEAD TO **EARTHQUAKES, TORNADOES,** AND EVEN **METEORS!**

JUST TO BRING UP SOME ENTIRELY HYPOTHETICAL EXAMPLES OF THE SORT OF APPALLING IGNORANCE WHICH I COULD **NEVER** CONDONE!

YOU ARE A SHINING LIGHT OF **REASON**, PAT ROBERTSON.

AT LEAST, ON **PARALLEL** EARTH.

*DID YOU SPOT THE **DIFFERENCE**? **PARALLEL** PAT ROBERTSON PARTS HIS HAIR ON THE **LEFT!** WEIRD, HUH?

TOM TOMORROW © 2010

THIS MODERN WORLD

by TOM TOMORROW

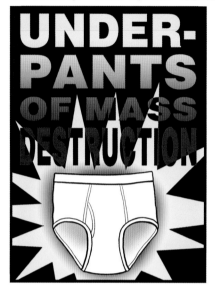

UNDER-PANTS OF MASS DESTRUCTION

EIGHT YEARS AFTER 9/11, THE LONG, STRANGE WAR ON TERROR GROWS EVER MORE SURREAL.

WE HAVE HUNDREDS OF THOUSANDS OF TROOPS OCCUPYING TWO COUNTRIES--PREDATOR DRONES "OPERATING" IN SEVERAL OTHERS--

--AND THEY HAVE... EXPLODING UNDERPANTS?

ADDITIONAL WARS ARE CASUALLY DISCUSSED!

PERHAPS WE WILL BE SAFER IF WE INVADE AND OCCUPY **YEMEN**!

WHAT THE HECK! IT'S WORTH A **TRY**!

CHRIS MATTHEWS FINDS IMAGINATIVE **NEW** THINGS TO WORRY ABOUT!

WHAT IF THE TERRORISTS KNOW **KUNG FU**? WHO CAN PROTECT US **THEN**?

RIGHT-WINGERS WANT TO KNOW WHY THE UNDERPANTS BOMBER WASN'T HAULED OFF THE PLANE AND **WATERBOARDED**!

HOW MANY TIMES DO WE HAVE TO **TELL** YOU PEOPLE? DUE PROCESS DOESN'T APPLY WHEN YOU'RE **VERY, VERY SCARED**!

THE THOUGHT OF THOSE TERRIFYING UNDERPANTS ALMOST MADE ME SOIL **MINE**!

(THEY HAVE APPARENTLY FORGOTTEN THAT THE **SHOE** BOMBER HAD A CIVILIAN TRIAL.)

DICK CHENEY ACCUSES OBAMA OF "TRYING TO PRETEND WE ARE NOT AT WAR."

AND WHO THE HELL ARE **YOU**?

I'M **YOUR** FUNDAMENTALLY ABSURD **IDEA** OF OBAMA-- AS DISTINCT FROM THE **REAL** OBAMA, WHO ESCALATES TROOP LEVELS AND BOMBS VILLAGES.

LIKE, PEACE, MAN.

AND THE T.S.A. CONTINUES **ITS** QUEST TO MAKE AIR TRAVEL AS UNPLEASANT AS HUMANLY **POSSIBLE**.

LADIES AND GENTLEMEN, NEW REGULATIONS REQUIRE THAT YOU BE **SEDATED** AND STRAPPED INTO YOUR SEATS LIKE **HANNIBAL LECTER** FOR THE DURATION OF TODAY'S FLIGHT!

YOUR UNDERPANTS WILL BE RETURNED TO YOU UPON ARRIVAL AT OUR DESTINATION.

TOM TOMORROW © 2010

THIS MODERN WORLD

by TOM TOMORROW

1969: OKAY, DIG IT! NO ONE KNOWS WE'RE SECRETLY RADICAL *LEFTISTS*! SO WE'RE GONNA *INFILTRATE* THE REPUBLICANS! WITHIN THREE OR FOUR DECADES, WE'LL BE IN *CHARGE*--AND THEN WE'LL DESTROY THE PARTY FROM *WITHIN*!

I WANT SOME O' WHAT *HE'S* SMOKIN'!

2008: MISSION *ACCOMPLISHED*, GENTLEMEN! AFTER EIGHT YEARS OF *OUR* STEWARDSHIP, THE G.O.P. IS DEMORALIZED AND SINKING IN THE POLLS--AND AMERICANS JUST ELECTED A PRESIDENT NAMED *BARACK HUSSEIN OBAMA*!

OUR WORK HERE IS *DONE*!

WE'LL LEAVE AGENT *PALIN* IN THE FIELD, JUST IN CASE.

BUT--BACK IN 1980: OKAY, SO, UH, CHECK IT OUT! NO ONE KNOWS WE'RE, UH, SECRETLY HARDCORE *RIGHT-WINGERS*! SO WE'RE GONNA *INFILTRATE* THE DEMOCRATS! WITHIN THREE OR, UH, FOUR DECADES WE SHOULD BE IN *CHARGE*--AND THEN WE'LL DESTROY THE PARTY FROM, UH, *WITHIN*!

WHAT AN *AUDACIOUS* PLAN!

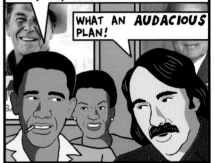

ONE THING, THOUGH--WE MAY HAVE A PROBLEM WITH YOUR *NAME*... "BARRINGTON CHADSWORTH IV" PROBABLY WON'T WIN OVER A LOT OF *LIBS*, WHEN THE TIME COMES...

WE'LL COME UP WITH SOMETHING MORE *MULTICULTURAL* FOR YOU... JUST MAKE SURE NO ONE *EVER* SEES YOUR ORIGINAL *BIRTH CERTIFICATE*!

NO PROBLEM! WHY WOULD ANYONE EVEN *WANT* TO?

PRESENT DAY: THE, UH, BUSH ADMINISTRATION COULDN'T HAVE LEFT THINGS IN WORSE SHAPE IF THEY'D, UH, *TRIED*...BUT ONE SHORT YEAR LATER, *DEMOCRATS* ARE DEMORALIZED AND SINKING IN THE POLLS--AND THE VOTERS OF MASSACHUSETTS JUST GAVE TED KENNEDY'S SEAT TO A *REPUBLICAN*!

YOU'VE DONE AN EXCELLENT JOB SO FAR, BARRINGTON-- ER, I MEAN, *BARACK*!

AT THE SAME MOMENT: DAMMIT, I THOUGHT WE WERE *DONE*! WHAT'S *WITH* THESE DEMS? WE GAVE THEM THE COUNTRY ON A SILVER PLATTER LAST YEAR! THEY COULDN'T HAVE BLOWN IT ANY FASTER IF THEY'D BEEN *TRYING*--

HEY, YOU DON'T SUPPOSE...

HMMMMM...

!?

UNDOUBTEDLY TO BE CONTINUED!

THIS MODERN WORLD

by TOM TOMORROW

Panel 1:
A SINGLE PAYER SYSTEM WOULD HAVE BEEN THE SIMPLEST SOLUTION.

IF WE COULD JUST REMOVE THE PARASITICAL *INSURANCE INDUSTRY* FROM THE EQUATION--

--THEN SOCIALISTS LIKE YOU WOULD *SEIZE POWER* AND *DESTROY AMERICA*--JUST LIKE GLENN BECK *WARNED* US!!

ER-- I-- WHAT?

CLEARLY THERE WAS NO HOPE OF *THAT*.

Panel 2:
THE NEXT BEST THING WOULD HAVE BEEN A PUBLIC OPTION, WHICH OBAMA SOMETIMES PRETENDED TO SUPPORT DURING THE CAMPAIGN.

BUT IF YOU GO BACK AND STUDY THE TRANSCRIPTS, YOU'LL SEE THAT I NEVER SPECIFICALLY USED THE WORDS "PUBLIC OPTION"!

SO WHEN I SAY NOW THAT I DID NOT *CAMPAIGN* ON THE PUBLIC OPTION--TECHNICALLY, I'M *ALMOST NOT LYING!*

Panel 3:
IN FEBRUARY, ROBERT GIBBS EXPLAINED THAT THE ADMINISTRATION WOULD NOT PURSUE A PUBLIC OPTION, DUE TO "VOTE COUNT" CONCERNS.

WE DON'T SEE *ANY POSSIBLE WAY* WE CAN GET 50 VOTES OUT OF THE, UM, 59 DEMOCRATS IN THE SENATE.

THAT DOESN'T MAKE ANY *SENSE*.

AND YOU'RE A CARTOON PENGUIN. NO ONE CARES WHAT YOU THINK.

THE WHITE H... WASHINGT...

Panel 4:
A MORE PLAUSIBLE EXPLANATION WAS SPELLED OUT PRETTY CLEARLY IN THE NEW YORK TIMES LAST AUGUST.

Several hospital lobbyists involved in the White House deals said it was understood as a condition of their support that the final legislation would not include a government-run health plan ..."We have an agreement with the White House that I'm very confident will be seen all the way through conference," one of the industry lobbyists told a Capitol Hill newsletter...

(full article: nyti.ms/a2PAXy)

Panel 5:
HIS SUPPORTERS LIKE TO CLAIM THAT THE PRESIDENT IS A MASTER TACTICIAN PLAYING A GAME OF MULTI-DIMENSIONAL *CHESS*...

HE'S SO FAR AHEAD OF EVERYONE ELSE, THE BRILLIANCE OF HIS STRATEGY WILL ONLY BE APPARENT IN *RETROSPECT!*

AND PERHAPS NOT EVEN *THEN!*

Panel 6:
BUT WHAT IF THE GAME IS *POKER*-- AND HE'S JUST A *LOUSY PLAYER*?

BEFORE WE START, UH, BIDDING, I THOUGHT IT ONLY FAIR TO SHOW YOU GENTLEMEN MY *CARDS!*

A VERY STRONG HAND INDEED, MR. PRESIDENT!

IF WE HAD ANY *SENSE*, WE'D FOLD RIGHT *NOW!*

HEH HEH!

HEH!

TOM TOMORROW © 2010

THIS MODERN WORLD

by TOM TOMORROW

Panel 1:

THE SUPREME COURT RULED THAT CORPORATIONS HAVE THE RIGHTS OF *CITIZENS*...BUT AN INJUSTICE *REMAINED*...

UM--WE WOULD LIKE THE RIGHT TO GET *MARRIED*...

NEVER MIND *YOU*! WHAT ABOUT THE RIGHTS OF *CORPORATE-AMERICANS*?

THEY DON'T EVEN HAVE *BODIES*!

Panel 2:

SCIENTISTS BEGAN TO GROW CLONED, CUSTOMIZED *AVATARS*, INTO WHICH THE COLLECTIVE CONSCIOUSNESS OF A CORPORATE ENTITY COULD BE *PROJECTED*...

THE...CREAMIEST DREAMIEST ICE CREAM MADE...LA LA LA LA LA LA LA...

I'VE DONE IT! IT'S ALIVE! IT'S *ALIVE*!!

Panel 3:

BEFORE LONG, CORPORATE-AMERICANS WERE EVERYWHERE...LIVING IN ORDINARY NEIGHBORHOODS...

HOWDY MISTER PFIZER! HOW ARE YOU TODAY?

FINE, BILL! SAY, I HOPE YOU DON'T MIND--I'M USING THE POWER OF EMINENT DOMAIN TO ANNEX YOUR *BACK YARD*!

I, UH-- WHAT?

Panel 4:

...RUNNING FOR PUBLIC OFFICE...

YOU CAN VOTE FOR POLITICIANS *FUNDED* BY ME--OR YOU CAN VOTE *DIRECTLY* FOR ME!

IT'S *ALWAYS* MORE EFFICIENT TO ELIMINATE THE *MIDDLEMAN*!

Panel 5:

...EVEN COMMITTING GRUESOME *CRIMES*!

SURE, I KILLED THE SMUG LITTLE TWERP! AND THANKS TO MY *LIMITED LIABILITY* AS A *CORPORATE*-AMERICAN, THERE'S NOTHING YOU CAN *DO*!

OUR MISTAKE THEN, SIR! SORRY TO BOTHER YOU!

Panel 6:

AND THEN THE FINANCIAL INSTITUTIONS REALIZED THEIR AVATARS COULD BE ANY *SIZE* THEY WANTED...

WE'RE *REALLY* TOO BIG TO FAIL NOW, GOLDMAN SACHS OLD CHUM!

INDEED WE ARE, CITICORP! SAY, PASS ME ANOTHER TAXPAYER, WOULD YOU?

I SWEAR, THEY'RE POSITIVELY *ADDICTIVE*!

TOM TOMORROW © 2010

THIS MODERN WORLD

by TOM TOMORROW

Panel 1:

AT THE TREEHOUSE HQ OF *CONSERVATIVE JONES*...

AH, MOONBAT--COME IN! YOU'RE UNDOUBTEDLY WONDERING ABOUT MY STRANGE *ATTIRE!*

ACTUALLY, I--

WELL YOU SEE, I'VE BEEN WORKING ON A CASE-- *UNDERCOVER!*

Panel 2:

BY CLEVERLY DISGUISING MYSELF AS A TELEPHONE *REPAIRMAN*, I WAS ABLE TO GAIN ACCESS TO THE OFFICE OF OUR LOCAL CONGRESSMAN...AND WHEN NO ONE WAS *LOOKING*, I SNUCK UNDER HIS DESK AND TIED HIS *SHOELACES* TOGETHER!

Panel 3:

WHEN HE TRIED TO STAND UP, HE FELL *FLAT ON HIS FACE!* AND *THAT* WAS WHEN I URINATED ALL OVER HIS *DESK!* IT WAS *BRILLIANT!*

I'VE GOT IT ALL ON VIDEO! IT'S UPLOADING NOW!

HUH. AND THE POINT TO ALL THIS WAS...?

Panel 4:

THE POINT WAS TO REVEAL THE *TRUTH*, MY DEAR MOONBAT! I AM A *CITIZEN JOURNALIST*-- AND IT IS MY NOBLE DUTY TO EXPOSE THE CONGRESSMAN AS A CLUMSY *OAF* WHOSE IDEAS DESERVE TO BE *URINATED* ON!

MAINSTREAM JOURNALISTS USE THESE TECHNIQUES ALL THE *TIME*, YOU KNOW!

UM--ARE YOU *SURE?*

Panel 5:

OH, MOONBAT! THE THINGS YOU DON'T UNDERSTAND ABOUT JOURNALISM COULD FILL A JOURNALISM *TEXTBOOK!*

SO WHAT BRINGS YOU UP TO THE TREEHOUSE, ANYWAY?

OH, *RIGHT*--I CAME UP TO TELL YOU--

Panel 6:

--THE *POLICE* ARE DOWNSTAIRS... THEY'D LIKE TO HAVE A *WORD* WITH YOU...

WHAT?! YOU KNOW WHAT THIS *MEANS?* THEY'VE COME TO *SILENCE* ME! TELL THE *WORLD*, MOONBAT! TELL THE WORLD MY *STORY!*

UH--SURE. I'LL GET RIGHT ON THAT.

NEXT TIME: THE MYSTERY OF AN INNOCENT CITIZEN JOURNALIST, UNFAIRLY PERSECUTED FOR *NO APPARENT REASON!*

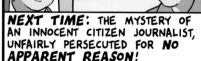

TOM TOMORROW © 2010

THIS MODERN WORLD

HEALTH CARE REFORMAGEDDON

THEY EXPECTED TO WIN THE DEBATE ON THE STRENGTH OF THEIR WELL-REASONED *ARGUMENTS.*

--AND IF ALL THESE WHINING SICK PEOPLE WOULD JUST *DIE*--THEY WOULDN'T *NEED* HEALTH CARE!

INDEED! YOUR LOGIC IS AS *IMPECCABLE* AS IT IS *IRREFUTABLE!*

WHY THANK YOU, MY GOOD SIR!

NO, NO-- THANK *YOU!*

OBAMA= HITLER

OBAMA= STALIN

ALAS, THEY WERE *WRONG*--AND ONE DAY AWOKE TO FIND THEMSELVES LIVING IN A SOCIALIST *NIGHTMARE!*

HOW *DARE* THEY STRIP ME OF MY RIGHT TO BE REJECTED BY AN INSURANCE COMPANY FOR PRE-EXISTING CONDITIONS!

THIS IS WHAT *TOTALITARIANISM* LOOKS LIKE!

GIVE OR TAKE.

SURE ENOUGH--THERE WERE GOVERNMENT AGENTS ON THEIR DOORSTEPS THAT VERY *DAY!*

HOWDY, MR. WILLIAMS! SAY, I'VE GOT YOUR *CENSUS* FORMS HERE!

UH HUH--AND HOW LONG DO I HAVE BEFORE YOUR *GOONS* HAUL ME OFF TO THE *GULAG?*

I, UH-- BEFORE WHO DOES WHAT TO THE *WHERE?*

THE HARDEST PART WAS EXPLAINING IT ALL TO THEIR CHILDREN.

MY DEAR SON--I AM SO SORRY YOU ARE GOING TO HAVE TO LIVE UNDER A SYSTEM IN WHICH YOU ARE, UM, LESS LIKELY TO BE REFUSED ACCESS TO HEALTH CARE!

BUT *WHY,* FATHER? WHY DID THE SOCIALISTS *DO* THIS TO US!?

AND NOW THEY MUST WORK TIRELESSLY--TO RESCUE THEIR NATION FROM THE ENEMIES OF *DEMOCRACY ITSELF!*

IT'S TIME FOR A *CIVIL WAR* IN THIS COUNTRY! AND I'LL DO *MY* PART--

--BY TWEETING "IT'S TIME FOR A CIVIL WAR IN THIS COUNTRY!"

THAT OUGHT TO GET THE BALL ROLLING!

TAP TAP TAP

TOM TOMORROW©2010

90

THIS MODERN WORLD

by TOM TOMORROW

THE TEXAS BOARD OF EDUCATION REWRITES HISTORY TO ITS OWN *LIKING*.

RATHER THAN "CAPITALISM"--LET'S CALL IT "THE ECONOMIC SYSTEM BESTOWED UPON MANKIND BY ALMIGHTY *GOD* IN HIS *INFINITE WISDOM*"!

I'D LIKE TO SEE MICHAEL MOORE TRY TO USE *THAT* IN A MOVIE TITLE!

I THINK WE SHOULD GIVE *THOMAS JEFFERSON* THE BOOT! THAT OLE BOY WAS PRACTICALLY A *MARXIST*!

MINOR ERRORS IN A REPORT ON CLIMATE CHANGE ARE SOMEHOW SUPPOSED TO DISCREDIT GLOBAL WARMING *ENTIRELY*.

NO ONE WHO *EVER* MAKES A MISTAKE, NO MATTER *HOW SMALL*, CAN EVER BE TRUSTED ABOUT *ANYTHING*!

LET ME SPELL IT *OUT* FOR YOU!

No Misteaks ALLOWED

CREATIONISTS USE GLOBAL WARMING SKEPTICISM TO BOLSTER THEIR *OWN* CASE.

SCIENTISTS CLEARLY HAVE *NO IDEA* WHAT THEY'RE TALKING ABOUT! THEY MADE THOSE MISTAKES IN THAT REPORT, AFTER ALL!

THEREFORE THE EARTH IS 6,000 YEARS OLD.

AND ADAM AND EVE RODE DINOSAURS.

AND THE WAR ON RATIONALITY MARCHES EVER ONWARD.

THE SO-CALLED LAWS OF AERODYNAMICS ARE JUST ANOTHER *HOAX* PERPETRATED BY EGGHEAD PROFESSORS AND THE ELITIST MEDIA!

AIRPLANES DO NOT "FLY"! THEY ARE HELD ALOFT THROUGH THE DIVINE INTERVENTION OF *HEAVENLY ANGELS*!

I'LL NOTIFY THE TEXAS BOARD OF EDUCATION AT *ONCE*!

TOM TOMORROW © 2010

THIS MODERN WORLD

by TOM TOMORROW

TOO MUCH CRAZY

1. SPEAKERS AT RIGHT-WING CONFERENCE READ TELEPROMPTER JOKES...OFF THE TELEPROMPTER.

HA HA I SEE WE HAVE OUR OBAMA COMMEMORATIVE TELEPROMPTER HERE TONIGHT!

HA HA

HA HA

HA HA I SEE WE HAVE OUR OBAMA COMMEMORATIVE TELEPROMPTER HERE TONIGHT

2. OBAMA D.O.J. CLEARS TORTURE MEMO AUTHORS OF PROFESSIONAL MISCONDUCT.

FINALLY! NOW, IF THE PRESIDENT NEEDS ANY ADVICE ON THE LEGALITY OF MASSACRING ENTIRE *VILLAGES* OR CRUSHING THE TESTICLES OF SMALL *CHILDREN*--TELL HIM TO GIVE ME A *CALL!*

DISTINGUISHED AND NOT AT ALL ETHICALLY CHALLENGED LAW PROFESSOR JOHN YOO

3. REPUBLICAN LAWMAKERS EXPRESS GUARDED SYMPATHY FOR GUY WHO FLEW PLANE INTO I.R.S. BUILDING.

"IT'S SAD THE INCIDENT IN TEXAS HAPPENED, BUT... (WHEN) WE ABOLISH THE I.R.S., IT'S GOING TO BE A HAPPY DAY FOR AMERICA!"
--REP. STEVE KING

"I CAN JUST SENSE NOT ONLY IN MY OWN ELECTION BUT SINCE BEING HERE IN WASHINGTON, PEOPLE ARE FRUSTRATED...NO ONE LIKES PAYING TAXES, OBVIOUSLY!"
--SEN. SCOTT BROWN

4. INFAMOUS ACORN TAPES TURN OUT TO HAVE BEEN MISLEADINGLY EDITED; MAINSTREAM MEDIA INEXPLICABLY RELUCTANT TO ISSUE CORRECTIONS.

"THE STORY SAYS O'KEEFE DRESSED UP AS A PIMP *AND* TRAINED HIS HIDDEN CAMERA ON ACORN COUNSELORS. IT DOES NOT SAY HE DID THOSE TWO THINGS AT THE SAME TIME."*

*ACTUAL EXPLANATION TO BLOGGER FROM NY TIMES PUBLIC EDITOR, PORTRAYED HERE AS A WEASEL.

5. CLIMATE CHANGE DENIALISTS CAN'T GET OVER THE FACT THAT IT STILL SNOWS IN THE WINTER.

WHERE IS THE YEAR-ROUND TROPICAL PARADISE IMPLIED BY THE PHRASE "GLOBAL *WARMING*"?

THANKS FOR *NOTHING,* AL GORE!

TOM TOMORROW©2010

THIS MODERN WORLD

by TOM TOMORROW

ALL THE RAGE

Panel 1:

RIGHT WING DISCOURSE IS DOMINATED BY PARANOID FANTASIES.

THE FIRST THING THE SOCIALISTS *DO* WHEN THEY TAKE OVER A COUNTRY--

--IS IMPOSE TEPID, INSURER-FRIENDLY *HEALTH CARE REFORMS!*

THEN THEY OPEN UP THE COAST TO OIL DRILLING.

IT'S A *FACT!*

Panel 2:

VIOLENT RHETORIC IS COMMONPLACE.

THE CRAZY *LIBERALS* SAY THAT I SHOULD TAKE IT DOWN A NOTCH! WELL YA KNOW WHAT *I* SAY?

LOCK AND *LOAD,* BABY! IT'S OPEN SEASON--ON *CRAZY LIBERALS!*

HA HA! JUST A HARMLESS *JOKE!*

LIBERALS HAVE *NO* SENSE OF HUMOR.

WINK!

Panel 3:

AND OF COURSE YOU'VE HEARD ABOUT THE RACIAL SLURS, DEATH THREATS, AND VANDALISM.

IN A DEMOCRACY SUCH AS OURS, ANY LAWMAKER WHO DOES NOT VOTE IN ACCORDANCE WITH THE WISHES OF A SMALL BUT OUTSPOKEN *CONSTITUENCY*--

--CAN EXPECT A BRICK THROUGH THE *WINDOW!*

JUST AS OUR FOUNDING FATHERS *INTENDED!*

Panel 4:

WE ALL KNOW WHERE THIS COULD EASILY LEAD--

--AND THIS JUST IN: THE INEVITABLE LARGE SCALE ACT OF RIGHT WING DOMESTIC TERRORISM HAS *FINALLY OCCURRED!*

WOW! NO ONE COULD HAVE *EVER* SEEN *THAT* ONE COMING!

Action McNews Network

Panel 5:

--AND WHO THE RIGHT WING WILL BLAME IF IT DOES.

THOSE GUYS WEREN'T *REALLY* TERRORISTS! OBAMA *MADE* THEM BLOW UP THAT BUILDING--

--WHEN HE SHOVED *HEALTH CARE* DOWN OUR THROATS!

DEMOCRATS ARE THE *REAL* TERRORISTS HERE!

YARGLE BARGLE!

BLARGH!

TOM TOMORROW © 2010

93

THIS MODERN WORLD

by TOM TOMORROW

IF REAL LIFE WERE MORE LIKE THE INTERNET

RANDOM STRANGERS WOULD HAVE VERY STRONG OPINIONS ABOUT YOUR EVERY SLIGHTEST MOVE.

LOOK AT THIS ASSCLOWN, WAITING FOR A *BUS!* WHAT IS HE, TOO STUPID TO *DRIVE?*

MAYBE HE'S *BRAIN DAMAGED,* EL-OH-EL!

ER--I-- WHAT?

A DISPROPORTIONATE NUMBER OF PEOPLE WOULD BE UNFAMILIAR WITH THE CONCEPT OF "EMPATHY."

HELP ME--I'VE BEEN *SHOT*--

HEY EVERYBODY! GET A LOAD OF THE *WHINGER!*

BOO HOO HOO! SOMEBODY CALL A *WAAHMBULANCE!*

EVERYONE WOULD EXPECT EVERYTHING TO BE FREE, AND EXCESSIVELY CONVENIENT.

HERE ARE THE *CHEETOS* YOU REQUESTED!

TOOK YOU LONG ENOUGH. SAY, WOULD YOU MIND CHEWING THEM UP AND SPITTING THEM INTO MY MOUTH FOR ME?

"ATTENTION" WOULD BE CONSIDERED AN ACCEPTABLE SUBSTITUTE FOR "MONEY."

WE'RE NOT GOING TO *PAY* YOU FOR FIXING OUR SINK--BUT WE *WILL* TELL OUR NEIGHBORS WHAT A GREAT JOB YOU DID!

THEN YOU CAN FIX *THEIR* SINKS.

?

ALSO FOR FREE.

YOU SHOULD SELL T-SHIRTS OR SOMETHING. I BET *EVERYBODY* WOULD BUY THEM!

AND OF COURSE, LIBERTARIANS WOULD BE THE DOMINANT POLITICAL FORCE IN AMERICAN SOCIETY.

I'M THE FIRST PRESIDENT IN HISTORY--WITH A *BLIMP!*

YES SIR. VERY GOOD, SIR.

Ron Paul

The New York Times

RON PAUL ELECTED I MASSIVE LANDSLIDE

Libertarian Majority in Congress Vow Tax-Free Utopia

TOM TOMORROW©2010

THIS MODERN WORLD

by TOM TOMORROW

Panel 1:
THERE EXIST AN INFINITE NUMBER OF *PARALLEL* WORLDS...ALL SIMILAR TO OUR OWN--BUT EACH WITH SOME CRUCIAL *DIFFERENCE*...

WORLD WHERE SARAH PALIN IS ASSISTANT MANAGER AT WASILLA WAL-MART.

WORLD WHERE GLENN BECK IS A SANE PERSON.

WORLD WHERE *GOOD* SPOCK IS THE ONE WITH A BEARD.

Panel 2:
ON ONE SUCH WORLD (AS ON OURS) A LOOMING SUPREME COURT VACANCY HAS INSPIRED MONTHS OF SPECULATION.

I WONDER IF PARALLEL OBAMA WILL NOMINATE A SAFE, TEPID *CENTRIST*--OR AN OUTSPOKEN, UNAPOLOGETIC *LIBERAL*!

YEAH, THE SUSPENSE IS JUST KILLING ME.

WHICHEVER WILL IT *BE*?

"SPUNKY," THE SARCASTIC TALKING PENGUIN OF *THIS* PARALLEL WORLD.

Panel 3:
NOW THE PARALLEL PRESIDENT HAS FINALLY ANNOUNCED HIS DECISION.

--AND SO I'M PLEASED TO PRESENT MY NOMINEE--A *BLANK SLATE* WHO HAS NEVER SO MUCH AS *UTTERED* A CONTROVERSIAL WORD!

THERE'S NO THERE *THERE*!

AT LEAST NOT THAT ANYONE'S GONNA *FIND*!

Panel 4:
THE CONSERVATIVE ATTACK MACHINE RESPONDS REFLEXIVELY, BUT WITH LITTLE APPARENT PASSION--

SO, UH, HOW DO WE KNOW THE BLANK SLATE ISN'T A FAR-LEFT RADICAL WHO WORSHIPS BILL AYERS AND SAUL ALINSKY AND, UH, YOU KNOW...ALL OF THAT...

BLAH BLAH BLAH, YADDA YADDA *YADDA*...

Panel 5:
--WHILE THE PARALLEL LEFT OCCUPIES A HOUSE *DIVIDED*.

OH WELL! IT'S *POLITICS*, AFTER ALL! I GUESS WE HAVE TO BE *REALISTIC*!

IF BY "REALISTIC" YOU MEAN "RESIGNED TO NEVER, EVER GETTING WHAT WE ACTUALLY WANT."

THAT IS PRECISELY WHAT I MEAN.

"SPUNKY" AGAIN.

Panel 6:
NEXT: THE SMALL, STUPID DETAIL AROUND WHICH THE ENTIRE CONFIRMATION PROCESS WILL ULTIMATELY REVOLVE.

ROBERT, IS THERE ANY TRUTH TO POLITICO'S REPORT THAT THE BLANK SLATE DOES NOT ENJOY *FRESH-BAKED APPLE PIE*?

LOOK--THE NOMINEE MAKES DESSERT-RELATED DECISIONS ON A *CASE-BY-CASE BASIS*!

PARA VHITE

THE PARALLEL WHITE HOUSE HAS NO FURTHER COMMENT AT THIS TIME.

...FORTUNATELY A POLITICAL SIDESHOW LIKE THAT COULD NEVER HAPPEN *HERE*!

TOM TOMORROW© 2010

THIS MODERN WORLD

by TOM TOMORROW

THANKS TO GLENN BECK--AND HIS CHALKBOARD--I'VE GOT YOUR NUM-BER *NOW!*

REALLY? DO TELL!

DON'T PLAY INNOCENT WITH *ME!* I KNOW ALL ABOUT YOUR CULT-ISH DEVOTION TO THE TEACHINGS OF YOUR GURU, *SAUL ALINSKY!*

EVERY DAY I ASK MY-SELF--*W.W.S.A.D?*

AND I KNOW ABOUT YOUR PLAN TO HASTEN THE COLLAPSE OF CAPITALISM VIA THE "CLOWARD-PIVEN STRATEGY," AS DETAILED IN A 1966 ARTICLE IN *THE NATION* MAGAZINE!

TALK ABOUT A HIDDEN MESSAGE!

I ALSO KNOW ABOUT THE SECRET PROGRESSIVE CONSPIRACY FOR WORLD DOMINATION DATING BACK TO THE ADMINISTRATION OF *WOODROW WILSON!*

WE PROGRESSIVE CON-SPIRACISTS DON'T LIKE TO *RUSH* THINGS.

MORE IMPORTANTLY, I KNOW ABOUT YOUR PLAN TO PROD TEA PARTIERS INTO ACTS OF VIOLENCE--WHICH WILL BE ENTIRELY *YOUR FAULT,* WHEN THEY OCCUR!

WHAT REASONABLE PERSON WOULD DARE TO SUGGEST *OTHERWISE?*

AND OF COURSE I KNOW ABOUT THE OODLES AND OODLES OF *SOROS MONEY* EVERYONE ON THE LEFT RECEIVES.

I KEEP MINE IN AN EMPTY SWIMMING POOL OUT BACK. WANT TO GO FOR A DIP?

YOUR MOCKERY IS STRAIGHT OUT OF THE *ALINSKY PLAYBOOK!*

DAMN! HOIST BY MY *OWN PETARD!*

THIS MODERN WORLD

by TOM TOMORROW

IF MORE BUSINESSES OPERATED LIKE GOLDMAN SACHS...

HERE'S THE PROTOTYPE OF OUR NEW PRODUCT, SIR!

WHAT DOES IT *DO*?

NOBODY REALLY *KNOWS*, SIR! IT'S TOO COMPLICATED TO UNDERSTAND, AND AS FAR AS WE CAN TELL, SERVES NO USEFUL PURPOSE WHATSOEVER.

OH, AND THERE'S A CHANCE IT WILL *EXPLODE* ONCE THE CONSUMER GETS IT HOME.

WELL, MAYBE MORE THAN A *CHANCE*.

ACTUALLY IT WAS DESIGNED BY A MUNITIONS EXPERT.

BUT NOT TO WORRY--*WE'RE COVERED!* UNBEKNOWNST TO THE CONSUMER, WE'LL BE TAKING OUT A *LIFE INSURANCE POLICY* ON EVERYONE WHO *BUYS* ONE OF THESE BAD BOYS!

SO WE'RE GOING TO CONVINCE OUR LOYAL CUSTOMERS TO PURCHASE A USELESS PRODUCT THAT WILL PROBABLY BLOW UP IN THEIR FACES--AND THEN PROFIT FURTHER WHEN IT *DOES*?

THAT PRETTY MUCH SUMS IT UP, SIR.

THE ONLY WORD FOR *THAT*--

--IS *FABULOUS!* LET'S GET IT INTO PRODUCTION *IMMEDIATELY!*

CAVEAT *EMPTOR*, THAT'S WHAT *I* SAY!

I COULDN'T AGREE *MORE*, SIR!

THREE YEARS LATER...

WHY *NO*, SENATOR-- IT NEVER *OCCURRED* TO ME THAT THE DEVICES WOULD *ACTUALLY EXPLODE!*

TOM TOMORROW © 2010

THIS MODERN WORLD

by TOM TOMORROW

A MASSIVE SPILL OF TOXIC RACISM THREATENS TO ENGULF THE AREA.

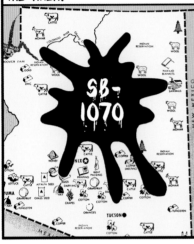

LOCAL AUTHORITIES TRY TO RE-ASSURE THE PUBLIC.

THERE CERTAINLY WON'T BE ANY *RACIAL PROFILING* GOING ON *HERE!*

HEAVENS NO! WE'LL *ALSO* BE ON THE LOOKOUT FOR ILLEGAL *CANADIANS!*

NOT TO MENTION *SWEDES!*

BUT THE REGIONAL ECONOMY COULD BE DEVASTATED.

BOYCOTT ARIZONA

BOYCOTT

BOYCOT

AND EXPERTS SAY THE DAMAGE WILL CONTINUE TO SPREAD.

AT LEAST *TEN OTHER STATES* ARE CONSIDERING SIMILARLY DRACONIAN IMMIGRATION LAWS!

THERE'S NO *TELLING* WHERE THIS MIGHT END!

THE FEDERAL RESPONSE SEEMS UNLIKELY TO CONTAIN THE PROBLEM.

WE PROPOSE A NATIONAL BIO-METRIC ID CARD--WHICH *EVERY* WORKER IN THE COUNTRY WOULD BE REQUIRED TO CARRY!

IT'S *ELEGANT* IN ITS NON-SIMPLICITY!

IN ANY CASE, MANY LOCAL RESIDENTS FEAR THEIR LIVES WILL NEVER BE THE SAME AGAIN.

SERIOUSLY? I HAVE TO BE READY TO PROVE I'M A CITIZEN EVERY TIME I WALK OUT THE *DOOR?*

SAY, DOESN'T THAT FELLA LOOK KINDA *CANADIAN?*

OR MAYBE *SWEDISH.*

TOM TOMORROW © 2010

THIS MODERN WORLD

by TOM TOMORROW

STEP ONE: PRIVATE INDUSTRY PUTS PUBLIC HEALTH AND/OR SAFETY AT RISK.

TO INCREASE THE EFFICIENCY OF OUR GRAVEL-MINING OPERATIONS, WE HAVE DEVELOPED A NEW CATEGORY OF EXPLOSIVE WE CALL THE *DOOMSDAY BOMB!*

A.K.A. THE *PLANET BUSTER!*

NOT TO WORRY! IT'S *PERFECTLY* SAFE!

World Wide Gravel

STEP TWO: WORRIED LIBERALS PROPOSE MODEST REGULATIONS.

IF WE'RE GOING TO ALLOW THEM TO DEPLOY THESE *DOOMSDAY BOMBS*--

--WE SHOULD AT *LEAST* REQUIRE THEM TO INSTALL A $1.97 CUTOFF SWITCH ON EACH DEVICE!

I MEAN--IT'S A *DOOMSDAY* BOMB!

STEP THREE: CONSERVATIVES PUSH BACK.

THIS IS AN *OUTRAGE!* DO YOU *REALIZE* HOW MUCH IT WOULD COST TO INSTALL THESE SO-CALLED SAFETY SWITCHES ON EACH DEVICE?

$1.97 *APIECE!*

EXACTLY!

STEP FOUR: MEDIA DUTIFULLY REPORT BOTH SIDES OF ISSUE.

THE WORLD SCIENTIFIC COMMUNITY HAS CONCLUDED THAT DOOMSDAY BOMBS ARE A DANGER TO ALL LIFE ON EARTH.

ON THE OTHER HAND, INDUSTRY-FINANCED SKEPTICS *DISAGREE!*

I GUESS THERE'S *NO WAY* TO KNOW WHO'S *RIGHT!*

Action McNews Network

STEP FIVE: INEVITABLE DISASTER UNFOLDS.

NO ONE COULD POSSIBLY HAVE PREDICTED THIS.

KA-BOOM!

STEP SIX: CONSERVATIVES DOUBLE DOWN ON THE CRAZY.

LIBERALS *WANTED* THIS TO HAPPEN--SO THEY'D HAVE AN EXCUSE TO IMPOSE MORE *REGULATIONS!*

ANYWAY--*I* THINK THERE ARE NUMEROUS *ADVANTAGES* TO OUR NEW *SUBDIVIDED* PLANET!

UM-- YOU'RE ON MY CHUNK.

WHAT?

Tom Tomorrow © 2010

100

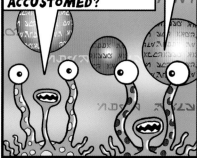

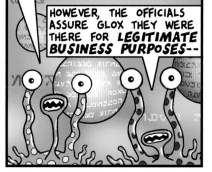
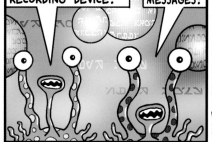

THIS MODERN WORLD

by TOM TOMORROW

Panel 1:

HELLO CHILDREN! I'M YOUR HOLO-GRAPHIC TEACHING INTERFACE, AND TODAY WE'LL BE STUDYING YOUR 21ST CENTURY *ANCESTORS*-- MORE COMMONLY KNOWN AS THE *WANKIEST GENERATION*--

--THE GENERATION *SO* APPALLING, HISTORIANS HAD TO COIN AN EN-TIRELY NEW ADJECTIVE JUST TO *DESCRIBE* THEM!

Panel 2:

AS YOU PROBABLY KNOW, THE WANKIEST GENERATION ARE RE-MEMBERED PRIMARILY FOR THE SHEER *IMMENSITY* OF THEIR SHORT-SIGHTED SELF-ABSORPTION!

FOR INSTANCE, IT IS DUE TO THEIR DITHERING AND OUTRIGHT *DENIAL* IN THE FACE OF ADVANCING GLOBAL *CLIMATE CHANGE*--

Panel 3:

--THAT YOU BOYS AND GIRLS AND SEXUALLY INDETERMINATE MUTATIONS ARE ONLY ALLOWED OCCASIONAL VISITS TO THE PLANET'S SURFACE-- IN THE BRIEF LULLS BETWEEN DEVASTATING CONTINENTAL *HELL-STORMS!*

BUT THAT'S ONLY *PART* OF THE WANKIEST GENERATION'S LEGACY!

Panel 4:

THEIR *ECONOMIC* INCOMPETENCE WAS AS STAGGERING AS IT WAS *IRRESPONSIBLE!* ADD IN THEIR PENCHANT FOR ENDLESS, POINTLESS *WARS*--AND THEIR WIDESPREAD ANTIPATHY TOWARD APPROPRIATELY PROGRESSIVE *TAXATION*--AND IT'S NO *WONDER* YOU CHILDREN WERE BORN 13 TRILLION DOLLARS IN DEBT--

--APIECE!

IT MAKES *ME* GRATE-FUL THAT I'M JUST AN A.I. SUBROUTINE!

Panel 5:

AND--YOU CHILDREN MAY NOT EVEN *KNOW* THIS, BUT ADULTS DID NOT *ALWAYS* LIVE IN FEAR OF BEING DECLARED *"UN-CITIZENS!"* BE-LIEVE IT OR NOT, THE "BILL OF CONDITIONAL PRIVILEGES" WAS ONCE KNOWN AS THE BILL OF *RIGHTS!"*

BUT YOUR ANCESTORS WERE AFRAID OF SO VERY MANY THINGS--DEMO-CRACY NEVER HAD A CHANCE OF SURVIVING *THEIR* STEWARDSHIP.

Panel 6:

AND OF COURSE WE CAN'T FORGET THE *TOXIC SLUDGE CONTAIN-MENT ZONES*--OR, AS THEY WERE KNOWN BEFORE YOU-KNOW-WHO GOT AHOLD OF THEM--*OCEANS!*

BUT YOU CHILDREN WILL LEARN MORE ABOUT *THAT* IN OUR *NEXT* LESSON!

AT LEAST, THOSE OF YOU WHO MAN-AGE TO *SURVIVE* ANOTHER WEEK!

BEST OF *LUCK!*

BUH-BYE!

TOM TOMORROW © 2010

THIS MODERN WORLD

by TOM TOMORROW

OBABA THE FAR-LEFT RADICAL AND A FEW OF THE FAR-LEFT RADICAL THINGS HE HAS DONE

1) PROLONGED WARS IN AFGHANI-STAN AND IRAQ; ORDERED PREDA-TOR DRONE ATTACKS IN PAKISTAN.

HEH HEH! I WILL CLEVERLY *PRETEND* TO SUPPORT ONGOING MILITARY ACTION--BY *SUPPORTING ONGOING MILITARY ACTION!*

SAUL ALINSKY WOULD HAVE BEEN SO *PROUD!*

(A DRAMATIZATION)

2) CRITICIZED "ACTIVISM" OF WARREN AND BURGER COURTS.

WHEN HE SAYS LIBERAL JUSTICES *OVERREACHED*--

--HE UNDOUBTEDLY MEANS THEY WERE EXCESSIVELY *UN-RADICAL* IN THEIR *NON-IMPLEMENTA-TION* OF AN EXTREMIST AGENDA SUCH AS HIS *OWN!*

WHAT OTHER POSSIBLE INTERPRETATION *IS* THERE?

3) EMBRACED BUSH POLICIES ON WIRETAPPING AND INDEFINITE DETENTION.

HIS CONTEMPT FOR THE CONSTITU-TION IS AN *OUTRAGE!*

SO AFTER SLEEP-ING THROUGH THE ENTIRE BUSH AD-MINISTRATION-- *NOW* YOU'RE SUD-DENLY A CIVIL LIBERTARIAN?

YEP! AND I WILL REMAIN SO, UNTIL THE MOMENT RE-PUBLICANS ARE SAFELY BACK IN POWER.

4) ANNOUNCED PLANS TO EXPAND OFFSHORE OIL DRILLING ONE MONTH BEFORE GULF BLOWOUT.

VERY SUSPICIOUS *TIMING,* IF YOU ASK *ME!* ALMOST AS IF HE *KNEW* HE WOULD NOT HAVE TO MAKE GOOD ON THAT PROMISE!

DOES *ACORN* HAVE A SECRET UNDER-WATER DEMOLITION TEAM?

JUST *ASKIN'!*

5) ANNOUNCED PLANS TO DEPLOY 1200 NATIONAL GUARD TROOPS TO U.S.-MEXICO BORDER.

HEH HEH! LITTLE DO CONSERVATIVES KNOW--I'M SECRETLY ORDERING THOSE TROOPS TO HELP ESCORT ILLEGALS *INTO* THIS COUNTRY!

EVERYTHING IS UNFOLDING EXACTLY AS WOODROW WILSON *PLANNED!*

(ALSO A DRAMATIZATION)

6) MOST DAMNING OF ALL--FAILED TO GOVERN IN ACCORDANCE WITH THE SPECIFIC WISHES OF THE *TEA PARTY!*

WE TOLD HIM WHAT *WE* WANTED DURING THE HEALTH CARE DEBATE--AND HE DID NOT *COMPLY!*

WHOEVER HEARD OF *PROTESTERS* BEING *IGNORED?*

ESPECIALLY WHEN THEY'RE *REAL* AMERICANS.

IF YOU, UH, KNOW WHAT I MEAN.

NEXT: UNDERMINING CAPITALISM--WITH THE HELP OF *TIMOTHY GEITHNER!*

TOM TOMORROW©2010

THIS MODERN WORLD

by TOM TOMORROW

INVISIBLE-HAND-OF-THE-FREE-MARKET-MAN

LOOK! UP IN THE **SKY**!

IF HE'S INVISIBLE, HOW COME WE CAN **SEE** HIM?

WHY MUST EVERYONE BE SO **PEDANTIC**?

SEVERAL WEEKS AGO: THE SITUATION IS GRIM AT THE B.P. COMMAND CENTER...WHEN SUDDENLY--

DESPAIR NO FURTHER, CITIZEN! I HAVE THE **SOLUTION** YOU NEED!

THAT'S **FANTASTIC**, I.H.O.T.F.M. MAN! WHAT'S YOUR **PLAN**?

WELL, THE FIRST THING WE'VE GOT TO DO IS CONTAIN THE TOXIC FLOW-- OF **INFORMATION!** WE'LL ENLIST LOCAL LAW ENFORCEMENT TO KEEP CAMERA CREWS AWAY FROM THE SPILL WHEREVER POSSIBLE! WE'LL FORCE CLEAN-UP WORKERS TO SIGN NON-DISCLOSURE AGREEMENTS--AND IF ANY OF THEM GET **SICK**, WE'LL BLAME IT ON **FOOD POISONING!**

THEN WE'LL SPEND $50 MILLION ON AN AD CAMPAIGN WITH PICTURES OF **PRISTINE BEACHES** AND **HAPPY PELICANS!** AND WE'LL BUY UP SEARCH ENGINE KEYWORDS-- AND THROUGH SURROGATES SUCH AS HALEY BARBOUR, WE'LL SUGGEST THAT MEDIA COVERAGE **OF** THE SPILL IS THE **REAL** CATASTROPHE!

AND THAT SHOULD PRETTY MUCH **DO** IT!

UH--BUT WHAT ABOUT THE LEAK ITSELF?

YOU SEEM TO HAVE ME CONFUSED WITH **TREE-HUGGING-ENVIRONMENTALIST-WACKO-MAN**.

I'M HERE TO SAVE THE **OIL INDUSTRY**--FROM THE PERILS OF **EXCESSIVE REGULATORY OVERSIGHT!**

THE **TAXPAYERS** CAN TAKE CARE OF THE MESS!

THAT'S HOW THE FREE MARKET **WORKS**, YOU KNOW!

WILL HE **SUCCEED**? STAY **TUNED!**

TOM TOMORROW ©2010

105

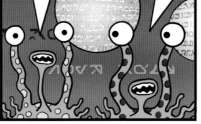

THIS MODERN WORLD

by TOM TOMORROW

THE SENSIBLE LIBERAL'S GUIDE TO SENSIBLE LIBERALISM IN THE AGE OF OBAMA

NOW FEATURING "CHUCKLES" THE SENSIBLE WOODCHUCK!

HOW MUCH WOOD **WOULD** A WOOD-CHUCK CHUCK, CHUCKLES?

NONE, IF HE WAS BUSY MARGINALIZING OBAMA'S LEFT-WING CRITICS **INSTEAD!**

EXCELLENT POINT.

SENSIBLE LIBERALS UNDERSTAND THAT THE PRESIDENT CAN'T GET EVERYTHING DONE **OVERNIGHT!**

I'M SURE HE'LL START TO GET US OUT OF IRAQ AND AFGHANISTAN **EVENTUALLY!** HE'S ONLY BEEN IN OFFICE A YEAR AND A HALF!

EVERYONE **KNOWS** YOU CAN'T CRITICIZE A PRESIDENT WHO'S ONLY BEEN IN OFFICE FOR A YEAR AND A **HALF!**

NOR CAN HE WAVE A MAGIC WAND AND MAKE ALL THE WORLD'S PROBLEMS SIMPLY **DISAPPEAR!**

AND ISN'T THAT **EXACTLY** WHAT HIS NAIVE, LEFT-WING DETRACTORS ARE **DEMANDING?**

THEY ARE SO FOOLISH, AND EASILY MOCKED! HAVE THEY EVER BEEN RIGHT ABOUT **ANYTHING?**

UH, LET'S NOT GO THERE.

SENSIBLE LIBERALS REALIZE THAT THE PRESIDENT DOESN'T REALLY HAVE MUCH POWER AT **ALL.**

ONLY A **CHILD** WOULD EXPECT HIM TO USE SOME SORT OF "BULLY PULPIT" TO "EXERT INFLUENCE" AND SOMEHOW "ACCOMPLISH THINGS"!

TRUE THAT! REMEMBER HOW MUCH TROUBLE **GEORGE BUSH** HAD GETTING ANYTHING **HE** WANTED?

THEY ALSO UNDERSTAND THAT INCONVENIENT FACTS ARE EASILY **IGNORED...**

THIS NUTCASE **BLOGGER** SAYS OBAMA ACTUALLY TRADED AWAY THE PUBLIC OPTION IN A BACK-ROOM DEAL AT THE VERY **START** OF THE HEALTH CARE DEBATE!*

LA LA LA LA LA I CAN'T **HEAARRRR YOOUUU!**

*AS DETAILED IN THE RELIABLY RADICAL NEW YORK TIMES.

...AND THAT **ANY** CRITICISM OF OBAMA CAN ONLY LEAD TO **ONE INEVITABLE OUTCOME.**

EITHER WE POLITELY OVERLOOK HIS RECORD ON HABEAS CORPUS, RENDITION, TROOP ESCALATION, PREDATOR DRONE STRIKES, WIRETAPPING, AND WHATEVER ELSE THESE WHINERS ARE COMPLAINING ABOUT--

--OR **SARAH PALIN** WINS IN 2012-- **GUARANTEED!**

BE **AFRAID!** BE **VERY AFRAID!**

BESIDES--ALL THAT STUFF IS **OKAY** IF YOU'RE A **DEMOCRAT!**

TOM TOMORROW ©2010

THIS MODERN WORLD

by TOM TOMORROW

TAKING AFGHANISTAN SERIOUSLY

ANOTHER IN AN OCCASIONAL SERIES OF CARTOONS ABOUT THINGS, AND TAKING THEM SERIOUSLY

SERIOUS: ASSESSING THE COST OF THE WAR AND DECLARING IT MONEY WELL SPENT.

$300 BILLION IS *CHUMP CHANGE*-- IF IT HELPS TO SOMEDAY POSSIBLY BEGIN THE PROCESS OF CONDITIONALLY BRINGING SOMETHING SORT OF RE-SEMBLING *STABILITY* TO THAT BELEAGURED NATION!

AS YOU WOULD UNDERSTAND, IF YOU WERE AS SERIOUS AS *ME*!

NOT SERIOUS: WONDERING IF THAT MONEY MIGHT HAVE BEEN PUT TO BETTER USE ELSEWHERE.

WITH OUR ECONOMY TANKING AND OUR INFRASTRUCTURE IN TATTERS, $300 BILLION SURE *SEEMS* LIKE A LOT TO HAVE WASTED ON AN INCREASINGLY POINTLESS WAR.

BUT WHAT DO *I* KNOW? I'M JUST A FRIVOLOUS *NINCOMPOOP*!

I WOULD PROBAB-LY HAVE SPENT IT ALL ON *ICE CREAM*!

SERIOUS: ACCEPTING THE RE-GRETTABLE NECESSITY OF AFGHAN CIVILIAN CASUALTIES.

SERIOUS PEOPLE UNDERSTAND THAT ACCIDENTS *HAPPEN* IN WARS!

YOU CAN'T MAKE A *FREEDOM OMELET* WITH-OUT BREAKING SOME *CIVILIAN EGGS*!

NOT SERIOUS: WONDERING HOW AFGHAN CIVILIANS FEEL ABOUT THAT.

IF *MY* WIFE OR CHILDREN WERE ACCIDENTALLY KILLED IN A PREDA-TOR DRONE STRIKE--I THINK I'D ACTUALLY BE PRETTY *UPSET*!

IF I WEREN'T SUCH A SCATTER-BRAINED *NINNY*, THAT IS!

LA LA LA LA LA LA LA!

SERIOUS: INSISTING THAT WE MUST STAY THE COURSE FOR AS LONG AS IT TAKES.

THE FACT THAT WE HAVE NOT ACHIEVED OUR OBJECTIVES AFTER NINE YEARS OF OCCUPATION--

--PROVES THAT WE MUST *EXTEND* THE OCCUPATION--*IN-DEFINITELY*!

IT'S THE ONLY *SERIOUS* THING TO DO.

NOT SERIOUS: WONDERING HOW LONG THAT WILL BE.

HOW MANY MORE TROOPS HAVE TO SACRIFICE THEIR LIVES BEFORE WE ARBITRARILY DECLARE VICTORY AND WITHDRAW?

WHICH IS, OF COURSE, HOW THIS INEVITABLY ENDS.

NOT THAT I WORRY *MY* EMPTY LITTLE HEAD ABOUT SUCH THINGS! IT'S ALL *MUCH* TOO COM-PLICATED FOR *ME*!

LA LA LA LA LA LA LA LA!

TOM TOMORROW ©2010

THIS MODERN WORLD

by TOM TOMORROW

RETIRE-MENT IS FOR LOSERS

A PUBLIC SERVICE MESSAGE FROM THE PRESIDENT'S BI-PARTISAN COMMISSION ON GUTTING SOCIAL SECURITY TO APPEASE THE DEFICIT HAWKS

FEATURING YOUR HOST CHUCKLES, THE SENSIBLE WOODCHUCK

MANY AMERICANS USED TO CONSIDER THEMSELVES *ENTITLED* TO A LEISURELY RETIREMENT.

I HAVE BEEN OPERATING THIS COMICALLY-OVERSIZED LEVER FOR 45 YEARS! MAY I HAVE MY *PENSION* NOW?

SHEESH! WHAT A *FREELOADER!*

(ARCHIVAL FOOTAGE)

BUT IN TODAY'S FAST-PACED WORLD, "OLD" IS THE NEW "YOUNG"!

MY HOUSE WAS FORECLOSED, MY 401(K) TANKED, AND WALL STREET *ATE* MY PENSION.

I HAVE NO CHOICE BUT TO WORK UNTIL I DIE.

IF THEY'LL *LET* ME.

THAT'S THE SPIRIT, OLD TIMER!

SO IT HARDLY EVEN *MATTERS* THAT WE'RE HOPING TO RAISE THE SOCIAL SECURITY AGE TO *SEVENTY** SOON!

WE CAN AFFORD ENDLESS WARS AND TRILLION-DOLLAR BAILOUTS--

--BUT *SOCIAL SECURITY* WILL *BREAK* US! SOMETHING MUST BE *DONE!*

MAKES SENSIBLE SENSE TO *ME!*

*FOR GEN X AND YOUNGER.

WHO EVEN *NEEDS* SOCIAL SECURITY--WHEN "NOT RETIRING" IS SHAPING UP TO BE *THE* HOT NEW TREND OF THE DECADE?

AND YOU'LL BE IN THE *VANGUARD*, YOU FABULOUS TRENDSETTER, YOU! ALONG WITH SUCH FAMOUS CELEBRITIES AS *RINGO STARR*, *BETTY WHITE*, AND *CLINT EASTWOOD!*

NOT TO MENTION *WILLIAM SHATNER!*

THEY NEVER RETIRED FROM *THEIR* JOBS--

--SO WHY ON EARTH SHOULD *YOU?*

UM--BECAUSE *I* WORK AT *WAL-MART?*

WHICH I'M SURE IS *EVERY BIT* AS *REWARDING*, IN ITS OWN WAY.

TOODLE-*OOO!*

NEXT: LAZY UNEMPLOYED PEOPLE WHO CAN'T *FIND* WORK--BECAUSE THEY ARE *LAZY!*

ALSO: 25 SURE-FIRE WAYS TO DISGUISE THE TASTE OF CAT FOOD, MORE OR LESS.

TOM TOMORROW©2010

THIS MODERN WORLD

by TOM TOMORROW

ON *OUR* EARTH, WINGNUTS PROFESS OUTRAGE OVER THE SO-CALLED "GROUND ZERO MOSQUE."

A VISITOR TO THAT HALLOWED GROUND *MIGHT* WANDER SEVERAL BLOCKS NORTH PAST THE NEIGHBORHOOD STRIP CLUBS, OFF TRACK BETTING PARLOR AND FAST FOOD JOINTS--AND STUMBLE ACROSS AN *ISLAMIC CULTURAL CENTER!*

I'M OFFENDED JUST *THINKING* ABOUT IT!

ON *PARALLEL* EARTH, THEY TAKE IT A STEP FURTHER.

YOU KNOW, THE WHOLE *ISLAND* OF MANHATTAN IS FULL OF MUSLIMS AND OTHER FOREIGN-LOOKING TYPES!

NOT TO MENTION *LIBERALS!*

THEIR VERY *PRESENCE* DEFILES THE MEMORY OF NINE-ELEVEN, IF YOU ASK *ME!*

PARALLEL POLITICAL OPPORTUNISTS ESCALATE THE CRAZY.

THIS BLASPHEMECRATION OF SACROSANCTIFIED GROUND IS *ABHORRENTIBLE!*

I REFUDIATE IT *UNEQUIVOCA-LUTELY!*

IT'S *SHOCKINGLY* INSENSITIVE! DON'T THESE NEW YORKERS UNDERSTAND WHAT GROUND ZERO MEANS TO *REAL* AMERICANS?

DEMOCRATS QUICKLY CAVE.

LET ME STATE CLEARLY THAT PEOPLE HAVE A RIGHT TO LIVE AND WORK IN MANHATTAN--

--BUT I'M NOT SAYING THEY *SHOULD.*

IT WOULD BE *BETTER* IF THEY LIVED AND WORKED ELSEWHERE.

AND EVENTUALLY...

I CAN'T *BELIEVE* THAT EVERYONE HAS TO ABANDON THE ISLAND OF MANHATTAN *ENTIRELY!*

WELL, IF SOME RIGHT WING NUTJOBS ARE OFFENDED--WHAT OTHER CHOICE DO WE *HAVE?*

LAST TRAIN OUT! ALL *ABOOOAAARD!*

NEXT: PARALLEL WINGNUTS FINALLY GET THE NEW YORK CITY OF THEIR DREAMS.

I *LOVE* NEW YORK LAND! IT'S SO CLEAN AND MONOCULTURAL!

THE BRAVERY OF THE AUDIO-ANIMATRONIC FIRST RESPONDERS IS *SO* INSPIRATIONAL!

CAN WE RIDE THE NINE-ELEVEN MEMORIAL *ROLLER COASTER?*

TOM TOMORROW ©2010

THIS MODERN WORLD

by TOM TOMORROW

SPARKY PREDICTS: BOGUS WINGNUT SCANDALS OF THE FUTURE

FUTURE EVENTS SUCH AS THESE **WILL** HAPPEN--

--IN THE FUTURE.

TRUST ME.

WITH A TIP O' THE PEN(GUIN) TO PANDAGON.NET

---

1) THERE WILL BE A SCANDAL ABOUT SOMETHING REALLY STUPID.

THE DAILY CALLER SAYS A PROMINENT LIBERAL IS MARRIED TO **ANOTHER** LIBERAL--AND THEY WON'T TELL **ANYONE** WHAT THEY DO IN BED!

WHAT ARE THEY TRYING TO **HIDE**?

I'LL BET THEY'RE HAVING SOME KIND OF WEIRD **LIBERAL SEX**!

WHATEVER THAT MIGHT BE.

---

2) A SCANDAL ABOUT SOMETHING BLOWN WAY OUT OF PROPORTION.

A LOW-LEVEL WHITE HOUSE STAFFER HAS A DISTANT RELATIVE WHOSE FRIEND'S NEIGHBOR'S BROTHER ONCE MADE A DISPARAGING REMARK ABOUT **RONALD REAGAN**!

SO IN OTHER WORDS, HATRED OF WHITE PRESIDENTS IS ENDEMIC AT THE **HIGHEST LEVELS** OF THE OBAMA ADMINISTRATION?

ISN'T THAT WHAT I JUST **SAID**?

---

3) A SCANDAL ABOUT SOMETHING EVEN **MORE** STUPID.

I WAS IN WASHINGTON D.C. FOR GLENN BECK'S RALLY--AND A LIBERAL ON THE SUBWAY LOOKED AT ME IN A **VERY** DISDAINFUL MANNER!

I BET HE WAS A MEMBER OF THAT **JOURNOLIST** YOU HEAR SO MUCH ABOUT!

---

4) A SCANDAL ABOUT SOMETHING WITH ABSOLUTELY NO BASIS IN REALITY.

A GUY ON THE INTERNET SAYS THAT MEXICAN DRUG GANGS ARE KIDNAPING TEXANS AND REPLACING THEM WITH **EXACT DUPLICATES** GROWN IN **PODS**!

IT'S ILLEGAL IMMIGRATION BY **STEALTH**!

NO **WONDER** OBAMA ISN'T DOING ANYTHING!

AND 5) A SCANDAL ABOUT SOMETHING SO BLATANTLY RACIST, IT JUST MAKES YOUR HEAD HURT.

OBAMA **KNEW** THAT A BLACK PRESIDENT WOULD POLARIZE THE COUNTRY--BUT HE RAN **ANYWAY**!

WHICH MEANS HIS ENTIRE PRESIDENCY IS A **DELIBERATE RACIAL PROVOCATION**!

IT'S ALL PART OF HIS PLAN TO IGNITE A **RACE WAR**!

I READ ABOUT IT ON THE INTERNET.

NEXT: SOMETHING MORE STUPID THAN YOU EVER IMAGINED POSSIBLE. **THEN**: SOMETHING MORE STUPID THAN **THAT**.

TOM TOMORROW ©2010

THIS MODERN WORLD

by TOM TOMORROW

THE RESPONSES WE GET: A BRIEF GUIDE

THE NITPICKER.
YOU MISSPELLED A WORD, NEGATING YOUR POINT, IF NOT YOUR *ENTIRE LIFE'S WORK!*

THE PEDANT.
THOUGH IT IS AN AMUSING IMAGE, IT IS NOT TECHNICALLY *TRUE* THAT POLITICIANS ARE ALIENS FROM ANOTHER PLANET WHO REQUIRE HUMAN BRAINS FOR NOURISHMENT.

THE NOOB.
WHAT *IS* THIS? YOU CALL THIS A *CARTOON?* WHY SO MANY *WORDS?* I HAVE NEVER BEFORE *SEEN* A CARTOON SUCH AS THIS!

THE EASILY BEFUDDLED.
WHAT DO YOU *MEAN* FOX NEWS HAS A RIGHT WING BIAS? I HAVE NEVER BEFORE *SEEN* THIS IDEA SUGGESTED!

THE SNOB.
NO ONE CARES WHAT A *CARTOONIST* THINKS! CARTOONS ARE FOR *CHILDREN!*

THE SCOLD.
THIS ISSUE IS NOT AS IMPORTANT AS *OTHER* ISSUES WHICH I BELIEVE YOU SHOULD BE WRITING ABOUT INSTEAD!

THE OSTRICH.
WHY DO YOU PAY ATTENTION TO RIGHT-WING CRAZIES? IF YOU WOULD JUST IGNORE THEM IN YOUR CARTOON, THEY WOULD *GO AWAY!*

THE CONCERN TROLL.
I AM A LIBERAL JUST LIKE YOU BUT I THINK YOUR CARTOONS ARE VERY MEAN TO REPUBLICANS AND YOU SHOULD STOP DRAWING THEM.

THE RIGHT-WINGER.
YOUR CARTOON SUCKS.

THE "TRICKY" RIGHT-WINGER.
YOUR CARTOON IS GREAT-- AT BEING *SUCKY!* HA HA! MADE YA LOOK!

THE VAGUELY DISSATISFIED.
THIS CARTOON IS NOT AS ENJOYABLE AS PREVIOUS CARTOONS I HAVE READ.

THE INCOMPREHENSIBLE LUNATIC.
YOUR CARTOONS ARE A PLAGUE UPON MANKIND, AND I DESPISE THE VERY GROUND YOU WALK ON YARGLE BARGLE *BLARRGH!*

AND THEN THERE'S *YOU*, DEAR READER--THE *SANE* ONE!
YEAH, *YOU!* THE ONE READING THIS! OBVIOUSLY NONE OF THIS APPLIES TO *YOU!*

HEH HEH!

TOM TOMORROW© 2010

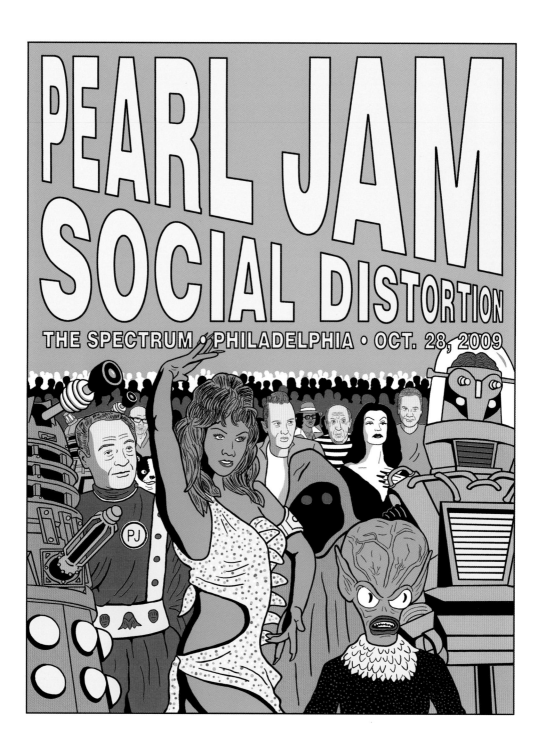

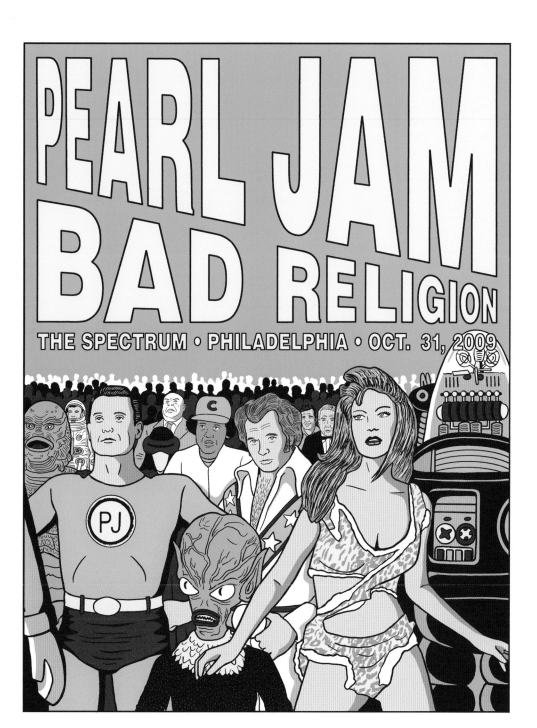

acknowledgments

Many thanks to my agent, Scott Moyers, and my editor Denise Oswald. They are the reason this book exists, and I am indebted to each of them.

Profound thanks to Eddie Vedder, Jeff Ament, Mike McCready, Stone Gossard and Matt Cameron—for trusting me as an artist, and for the all-encompassing trip which ensued. Thanks also to Tim Bierman, Kelly Curtis, Andy Fischer, and everyone at Ten Club—it was great working with all of you.

Most of all, I owe sincere and heartfelt thanks to every editor who continues to run my work each week. Without them, these cartoons would never have been written.

Onstage with Pearl Jam, May 2010. I'm the one who looks like a cartoonist.

TOM TOMORROW is the creator of the nationally syndicated political cartoon, *This Modern World*, which appears each week at Salon.com, and in alternative papers around the country. His work has also been featured in *The New York Times*, *US News & World Report*, *The New Yorker*, *The American Prospect*, *The Nation*, *Spin*, *Esquire*, and on MSNBC's *Countdown with Keith Olbermann*. A two-time recipient of the Robert F. Kennedy Journalism Award for Cartooning, Tom Tomorrow is the author of eight cartoon compilations and one book for children.